MW00324983

Frederick Seidel New Selected Poems

ALSO BY FREDERICK SEIDEL

Peaches Goes It Alone

Widening Income Inequality

Nice Weather

Poems 1959–2009

Evening Man

Ooga-Booga

The Cosmos Trilogy

Barbados

Area Code 212

Life on Earth

The Cosmos Poems

Going Fast

My Tokyo

These Days

Poems, 1959–1979

Sunrise

Final Solutions

Frederick

Seidel

New

Selected

Poems

faber

First published in the UK in 2021
by Faber & Faber Ltd
Bloomsbury House
74–77 Great Russell Street
London WC1B 3DA

First published in the US in 2020
by Farrar, Straus and Giroux
120 Broadway, New York 10271

Designed by Richard Oriolo
Printed in the UK by TJ Books Ltd, Padstow, Cornwall

All rights reserved
© Frederick Seidel, 2020, 2021

The right of Frederick Seidel to be identified as author of this work
has been asserted in accordance with Section 77 of the Copyright,
Designs and Patents Act 1988

A CIP record for this book is available from the British Library

ISBN 978–0–571–36535–7

FSC
www.fsc.org
MIX
Paper from
responsible sources
FSC® C013056

2 4 6 8 10 9 7 5 3 1

TO JONATHAN GALASSI

AND TENOCH ESPARZA

Contents

From

Sunrise

(1980)

1968

A football spirals through the oyster glow
Of dawn dope and fog in L.A.'s
Bel Air, punted perfectly. The foot
That punted it is absolutely stoned.

A rising starlet leans her head against the tire
Of a replica Cord,
A bonfire of red hair out of
Focus in the fog. Serenading her,
A boy plucks "God Bless America" from a guitar.
Vascular spasm has made the boy's hands blue
Even after hours of opium.

Fifty or so of the original
Four hundred
At the fundraiser,
Robert Kennedy for President, the remnants, lie
Exposed as snails around the swimming pool, stretched
Out on the paths, and in the gardens, and the drive.
Many dreams their famous bodies have filled.

The host, a rock superstar, has
A huge cake of opium,
Which he refers to as "King Kong,"
And which he serves on a silver salver
Under a glass bell to his close friends,
So called,
Which means all mankind apparently,
Except the fuzz,
Sticky as tar, the color of coffee,
A quarter of a million dollars going up in smoke.

This is Paradise painted
On the inside of an eggshell
With the light outside showing through,
Subtropical trees and flowers and lawns,
Clammy as albumen in the fog,
And smelling of fog. Backlit
And diffuse, the murdered
Voityck Frokowski, Abigail Folger and Sharon Tate
Sit together without faces.

This is the future.
Their future is the future. The future
Has been born,
The present is the afterbirth,
These bloodshot and blue acres of flowerbeds and stars.
Robert Kennedy will be killed.
It is '68, the campaign year—
And the beginning of a new day.

People are waiting.
When the chauffeur-bodyguard arrives
For work and walks
Into the ballroom, now recording studio, herds
Of breasts turn round, it seems in silence,
Like cattle turning to face a sound.
Like cattle lined up to face the dawn.
Shining eyes seeing all or nothing,
In the silence.

A stranger, and wearing a suit,
Has to be John the Baptist,
At least, come
To say someone else is coming.
He hikes up his shoulder holster
Self-consciously, meeting their gaze.
That is as sensitive as the future gets.

THE SOUL MATE

Your eyes gazed
Sparkling and dark as hooves,
They had seen you through languor and error.
They were so still. They were a child.
They were wet like hours
And hours of cold rain.

Sixty-seven flesh inches
Utterly removed, of spirit
For the sake of nobody,
That one could love but not know—
Like death if you are God.
So close to me, my soul mate, like a projection.

I'd loved you gliding through St. Paul's sniffing
The torch of yellow flowers,
The torch had not lit the way.
Winter flowers, yourself a flame
In winter. In the cold
Like a moth in a flame.

I seemed to speak,
I seemed never to stop.
You tossed your head back and a cloud
Of hair from your eyes,
You listened with the beautiful
Waiting look of someone

Waiting to be introduced,
Without wings but without weight, oh light!
As the fist which has learned how
Waving goodbye, opening and closing up to the air
To breathe. The child
Stares past his hand. The blank stares at the child.

Goodbye.

SUNRISE

FOR BLAIR FOX

The gold watch that retired free will was constant dawn.
Constant sunrise. But then it was dawn. Christ rose,
White-faced gold bulging the horizon
Like too much honey in a spoon, an instant
Stretching forever that would not spill; constant
Sunrise blocked by the buildings opposite;
Constant sunrise before it was light. Then it
Was dawn. A shoe shined dully like liquorice.
A hand flowed toward the silent clock radio.

Bicentennial April, the two hundredth
Lash of the revolving lighthouse wink,
Spread out on the ceiling like a groundcloth.
Whole dream: *a child stood up*. Dream 2: *yearning,*
Supine, head downhill on a hill. Dream: *turning*
And turning, a swan patrols his empty nest,
Loops of an eighteenth-century signature, swan crest,
Mother and cygnet have been devoured by the dogs.
The dogs the dogs. *A shadow shivered with leaves*.

Perth, Denpasar, Djakarta, Bangkok, Bom
Bombom bay. Dogs are man's greatest invention. Dogs.
They were nice dogs. Find a bottle of Dom
Pérignon in Western Australia.
Find life on Mars. Find Jesus. "You are a failya,"
The president of the United States said.
He was killed, and she became Bob's. His head,
Robert Kennedy's, lay as if removed
In the lap of a Puerto Rican boy praying.

Ladies and gentlemen, the president
Of the United States, fall in the air,
A dim streetlight past dawn not living to repent,
Ghostwalks by the canal, the blood still dry
Inside soaked street shoes, hands washed clean that try
To cup the rain that ends the drought. No one
Spoke. Blindfolds, plus the huge curtains had been drawn.
Because of his back he had to be on his back.
Neither woman dreamed a friend was the other.

Innocence. Water particles and rainbow
Above the sweet smell of gasoline—hiss of a hose
Drumming the suds off the town car's whitewalls, which glow!
Pink-soled gum boots, pink gums of the ebony chauffeur,
Pink summer evenings of strontium 90, remember?
Vestal black panther tar stills the street.
The coolness of the enormous lawns. Repeat.
O innocent water particles and rainbow
Above the sweet smell of gas, hiss of the hose!

When you are little, a knee of your knickers torn,
The freshness of rain about to fall is what
It would be like not to have been born.
Believe. Believed they were lined up to take showers
Dies illa, that April, which brought May flowers.
Safer than the time before the baby
Crawls is the time before he smiles, maybe.
Stalin's merry moustache, magnetic, malignant,
Crawls slowly over a leaf which cannot move.

If the words sound queer and funny to your ear,
A little bit jumbled and jivey, it must be
Someone in 1943 you hear:
Who like a dog looking at a doorknob
Does not know why. Slats of daylight bob
On the wall softly, a gentle knocking, a breeze.
A caterpillar fills the bed which is
Covered with blood. 1943.
The stools in the toilet bowl, are they alive?

Harlem on fire rouged the uptown sky.
But the shot squeezed off in tears splashes short.
But bullets whizzing through hell need no alibi
Before they melt away. Intake. Compression,
Ignition, explosion. Expansion. Exhaust. Depression
Reddens the toilet paper. That black it feels.
Endomorphic round-fendered automobiles
Slow, startle each other, and bolt in herds across
Spuyten Duyvil for the fifties and Westchester.

The cob stayed on the pond, perfect for Westchester,
Circling a nonexistent pen. Polly
Urethane sat on his face, Polly Esther
Sat on his penis. Protecting the non-cygnet.
Walking one day through the Piney Woods, he met
Three dogs in that peculiar light, strays. Two
Were shitting, looking off in that way dogs do,
Hunchbacked, sensitive, aloof, and neither
Male nor female. The third sat licking its teeth.

At the Institute they are singing *On Human
Symbiosis and the Vicissitudes
of Individuation*. Light of the One—
A summer sidewalk, a shadow shivered with leaves.
The mother smiles, *fa, so,* the mother grieves,
Beams down on the special bed for spinal
Injuries love that is primary and final,
Clear crystal a finger flicked that will ring a lifetime.
Plastic wrap refuse in the bare trees means spring.

And clouds blowing across empty sky.
A gay couple drags a shivering fist-sized
Dog down Broadway, their parachute brake. "Why
Robert Frost?" the wife one pleads, nearly
In tears; the other sniffs, "Because he
Believed in Nature and I believe in Nature."
Pacing his study past a book-lined blur,
A city dweller saw breasts, breast; their sour
And bitter smell is his own smoker's saliva.

The call had finally arrived from Perth:
He would live. C-4, a very high cervical
Lesion, but breathing on his own—rebirth
Into a new, another world, just seeing,
Without losing consciousness, and being,
Like being on the moon and seeing Earth,
If you could breathe unaided. God, in Perth,
Twelve hours' time difference, thus day for night,
It was almost winter and almost Easter.

So accepting life is of the incredible.
2 a.m., the reeking silky monsoon
Air at Bombay Airport is edible,
Fertile, fecal, fetal—thunder—divine
Warm food for Krishna on which Krishna will dine.
The service personnel vacuum barefooted,
Surely Untouchables. Thunder. The booted
Back down the aisles spraying disinfectant,
By law, before disembarkation in Perth.

Down Under thunder thunder in formation
Delta wing Mach 2 dots time-warp to dust
Motes, climb and dissolve high above the one
Couple on the beach not looking up,
In the direction of Arabia, Europe,
Thunder, thunder, military jets,
Mars. The man smokes many cigarettes.
The man was saying to the woman, "Your son
Has simply been reborn," but can't be heard.

All is new behind their backs, or vast.
House lots link up like cells and become house,
Shade tree and lawn, the frontier hypoblast
Of capitalism develops streets in minutes
Like a Polaroid. The infinite's
Sublime indifference to the mile—Mao
On nuclear war. Inches; dust motes; they go bow wow
At the heels of history. The dust
Imitates the thunder that will bring rain.

By the Indian Ocean, he sat down
And wept. Snarl suck-suck-suck waaah. It was the Grand
Hôtel et de Milan. It was a gown
Of moonlight, moving, stirring a faint breeze,
Gauze curtains hissing softly like nylons please
Please crossing and uncrossing. Who—how had
The shutters opened? and the heavy brocade
Curtain? How far away the ceiling was.
The bedlamp. One floor below, Verdi died.

How far away Australia was, years.
A man asleep listened while his throat
Tried to cry for help. He almost hears
The brayed, longing, haunting whale song the deaf speak,
Almost words. Out of silence, sounds leak
Into silence, years. He lay there without
Love, in comfort, straining to do without,
And dreamed. A spaceship could reach the ceiling, the special
Theory of relativity says.

Leave love, comfort, not even masturbate,
Not even love justice, not even want to kill,
O to be sterile, and to rise and wait
On the ceiling at sunrise, for dawn! stainless blond
Ceiling, the beginning of the beyond!
But the TV showed outstretched hands—a revolver
Blocked the open door of the last chopper,
Struggling to get airborne. The ditto sheet served
With espresso began: *Good morning! Here are the news.*

Phosphorescent napkins don't make a bomb;
Under the parasols of Bicè's, Via
Manzoni, chitchat chased the firefly of Vietnam.
The courtyard flickered; the tablecloth glowed like lime.
Corrado Agusta's chow chow took its time
Turning its head to look at one, very
Refined and inhuman and dark as a mulberry,
Not a dog. Its blue tongue was not on view.
It had a mane and wore a harness, unsmiling.

Being walked and warmed up, they roared like lions on leashes.
The smell of castor oil. Snarl suck-suck-suck waaah
A racing motorcycle running through
The gears, on song; the ithyphallic faired
Shape of speed waaah an Italian's glans-bared
Rosso di competizione. The Counts
Agusta raced these Stradivarius grunts
As genteelly as horse farms race horses—helicopter
Gunships, Agusta Aeronautiche.

The communists organized. Domenico
Agusta reigned. Of course the one who knew
Kennedys was the cold white rose Corrado.
The boss nailed each picket by name with a nod,
While Ciudad Trujillo and Riyadh
Kept unrolling more terror dollars for Corrado.
The iron and pious brother saw God go;
The salesman brother settled for everything:
Small arms fire, new nations; splits of brut, dry tears.

Domenico Agusta saw God go
Backwards like a helicopter in
A film he saw in Rome—i.e., in tow
With a helicopter. Sunbathers on Rome's
Roofs looked sideways from their cradled arms.
Just outside the window Jesus appears.
He faces us and steadily disappears.
The audience applauded. So odd to be
Agusta lifting off in your Agusta.

Goodbye. Goodbye. The stuck door was freed
And thrown open, and then closed and sealed.
The moviegoers of the world recede,
The White House and the tiny Marine band
Were wheeled away. A bulbously gloved hand
Frees the faulty door. Thrown open. Into
The countdown, and counting. *−9*. When you
Are no longer what you were. Thrown open.
−8. O let me out nor in.

Forty stories stock still like a boy
Whose height is being measured stands on smoke
As they withdraw the gantry, wheeled awoy,
Away. Perth Denpasar Djakarta Bangkok
Bombay in the capsule at the extreme tock,
La la, in the minute head above
The rest, eye movement peck peck like a dove,
A man sits on his back strapped down reading
Off numbers and getting younger, counting, cooing.

Millions of pounds of propellants make one dream,
Even more than psychoanalysis,
Of getting somewhere. Eyes glow in the gleam
Of the fuel gauges. Liquid oxygen
And kerosene. Check. Liquid oxygen
And liquid hydrogen—liquid in a freeze
Of −420°
F. Smoke boils off the ice that sheathes
The stainless steel building beneath him, forty floors.

Blue as the winder sapphire of the Cartier
Watch he has no use for now, goodbye,
The diodes of the digital display—
Information the color of his eyes,
As if his life were passing before his eyes,
—7. *Fin de race* face Louis
Cartier designed, inside a chewy
Candy of gold; face in a diver's helmet
Glassed in, prickles of the gold rivets and screws.

For everyday use, but by a Tutankhamen.
It would look feminine on a girl. The first
Wristwatch amused the sports of 1907.
The sport who commissioned the original,
The Brazilian Santos-Dumont, for a while
In 1906 believed he was the first man
To fly. Who says he did? None other than
The National Air and Space Museum says
Fernando Hippolyto da Costa does—

Believes Santos *was*. How could—but then
Who cares? Santos did not. Santos was not.
The watch was 1908, some say seven.
—6. What is there to believe in?
—6. What kind of god is not even
Immortal! —6. Nothing lasts.
A block of hieroglyphics trumpets, blasts
A golden long upended riff of silence,
It says for whom, whose name has been effaced.

To speak the name of the dead is to make them live
Again. O pilgrim, restore the breath of life
To him who has vanished. But the names they give.
No one can pronounce the hieroglyphs.
Then they had vowels to breathe with their bare midriffs,
Yes which? No one's known how to vocalize
The consonants. The kings don't recognize
Their names, don't recognize our names for them;
The soft parts that could not be embalmed are life.

One simply stares at the autistic face,
Charred rock-hard paper, a god. Stares at the stared-at.
Ramesses II in an exhibit case.
The Mummy Room is packed with Japanese
And German tours there to take in Ramesses.
The guides call in their languages, "This way please."
It seems one stares until one hardly sees.
It seems the room is empty. Like a dog
Looking at a doorknob, one stares at the stared-at.

As at a beetle rolling a ball of dung.
As at a large breast, with its nipple erect.
—5, soft and hard together among
The million things that go together one
Will lift away from, everything under the sun,
Everything—dog and doorknob—combustion to vapor
Lock—scissors cut paper, rock breaks scissors, paper
Covers rock. Everything is looking
For something softer than itself to eat.

Think of the energy required to get
Away from this hunt and peck for energy
That's running out. This need to look! O let
Your spirit rise above the engines below you.
Prepare for launch. O let a new way know you
Helmeted and on your back strapped down.
The moisture of the viscera, the blown
Coral rose of the brain on its stem—in this
Container, soft will never be exposed.

And leave behind the ancient recipes,
That cookbook for cannibals the Old Testament,
Bloody contemporary of course of Ramesses.
Cuisine minceur, urging one to eat less
But well. O Egypt! O Israel's salt sweetness!
From going soft and hard, from going up
And down, deliver us: struggling up
The steep path as Abraham with fire and knife,
And struggling down as Moses bent under the Law.

O let me go. O Israel! O Egypt!
The enemy's godless campfire at night, meat roasting
As you breathed near, sword drawn. *Cut.* Juice that dripped—
Later—from the dates from the hand of your daughter
Placed on your tongue in joy. Salute the slaughter.
O let me go. Salute the screenwriter,
DNA. Salute the freedom fighter
Kalashnikov machine pistol. A spider
Oiling the weapon spreads its legs and sighs.

TERROR OUR PLEASURE. O let me go. Logo
Of the age of ass—this age of movements—
Members and dismembers is our motto.
Oiling her weapon while in the mirror eyeing
Herself, turbaned in a black howli, sighing,
Is our muse *It feels good*, the spider. Mothers,
The children must die with dignity. Brothers,
Die. Mothers, calm the children. Squirt the poison
Far back in your child's throat. Stanza thirty-five.

Seated on your back strapped tight, tighter,
Feeling the contoured chair's formfitting
Love—no more hunt and peck on the typewriter
For energy that's running out. Stable
Fireproof love ideally comfortable!
You stare up at the gauges' radiance.
The mummy priest stares back in a trance,
And places beside you the silent clock radio,
And on the floor shoes for the long journey.

To lie on the horizon unable to rise—
How terrible to be the horizon! be
The expression in the quadriplegic's eyes,
Constant sunrise of feelings but no feeling.
The patient on the couch cow-eyes the ceiling.
Under his broken armor is a flower
Pinned down, that cannot reach its dagger, a flower.
Tongs in his skull, and dreams, not every man
Will wake. Can stand to look down at his penis and urine.

I am less than a man and less than a woman,
Wave after wave of moonlight breaks
On the trembling beach, dogs howl everywhere. One
Heave, and the water of the swimming pool
Sprang up, turning on its side like a pole-
Vaulter as it rose −4
In impossible slow motion. Whisper. Roar.
Because the stirred-up air only smells sweeter.
Because on Bali the earthquake toll is this sweet.

The Ketjak dancers roar and whisper *ketjak*
In ecstasy, the monkey dancers, k-*tchuck*.
They sway, but stayed seated, *ketjak*, *ketjak*.
−3, C-4, we have ignition.
Lit up, the streets of Cairo are singing of urine,
The streets of Bombay are quiring human faeces.
−2 is the sea anemones
Which elsewhere are galaxies. Time-space is the amoeba's
Pouring motion into itself to move.

Organizations of gravity and light,
Supremely mass disappears and reappears
In an incomprehensible —*i* of might.
Sat up at last, the quadriplegic boy
Feels beyond pain, feels beyond joy—
Still, stately as the Christ of Resurrection.
I wake beneath my hypnopompic erection,
Forty stanzas, forty Easters of life,
And smile, eyes full of tears, shaking with rage.

TO ROBERT LOWELL AND
OSIP MANDELSTAM

I look out the window: spring is coming.
I look out the window: spring is here.
The shuffle and click of the slide projector
Changing slides takes longer.

I like the dandelion—
How it sticks to the business of briefly being.
Shuffle and click, shuffle and click—
Life, more life, more life.

The train that carried the sparkling crystal saxophone
Osip Mandelstam into exile clicketyclicked
Through suds of spring flowers,
Cool furrowed-earth smells, sunshine like freshly baked bread.

The earth was so black it looked wet,
So rich it had produced Mandelstam.
He was last seen alive
In 1938 at a transit camp near Vladivostok

Eating from a garbage pile,
When I was two, and Robert Lowell was twenty-one,
Who much later would translate Mandelstam,
And now has been dead two years himself.

I sometimes feel I hurry to them both,
Stand staring at the careworn spines
Of their books in my bookshelf,
Only in order to walk away.

The wish to live is as unintentional as love.
Of course the future always is,
Like someone just back from England
Stepping off a curb, I'll look the wrong way and be nothing.

Heartbeat, heartbeat, the heart stops—
But shuffle and click, it's spring!
The arterial branches disappearing in the leaves,
Swallowed like a tailor's chalk marks in the finished suit.

We are born.
We grow old until we're all the same age.
They are as young as Homer whom they loved.
They are writing a letter, not in a language I know.

I read: "It is one of those spring days with a sky
That makes it worthwhile being here.
The mailbox in which we'll mail this
Is slightly lighter than the sky."

MEN AND WOMAN

Her name I may or may not have made up,
But not the memory,
Sandy Moon with her lion's mane astride
A powerful motorcycle waiting to roar away, blipping
The throttle, a roar, years before such a sight
Was a commonplace,
And women had won,

And before a helmet law, or
Wearing their hair long, had made all riders one
Sex till you looked again; not that her chest
Wasn't decisive—breasts of Ajanta, big blue-sky clouds
Of marble, springing free of her unhooked bra
Unreal as a butterfly-strewn sweet-smelling mountainside
Of opium poppies in bloom.

It was Union Square. I remember. Turn a corner
And in a light-year
She'd have arrived
At the nearby inky, thinky offices of *Partisan Review*.
Was she off to see my rival Lief,
Boyfriend of girls and men, who cruised
In a Rolls convertible?

The car was the *caca* color a certain
Very grand envoy of Franco favored for daytime wear—
But one shouldn't mock the innocent machinery
Of life, nor the machines we treasure. For instance,
Motorcycles. What definition of beauty can exclude
The MV Agusta racing 500-3,
From the land of Donatello, with blatting megaphones?

To see Giacomo Agostini lay the MV over
Smoothly as a swan curves its neck down to feed,
At ninety miles an hour—entering a turn with Hailwood
On the Honda, wheel to wheel, a foot apart—
The tromboning furor of the exhaust notes as they
Downshifted, heard even in the photographs!
Heroes glittering on the summit before extinction

Of the air-cooled four-strokes in GP.
Agostini—Agusta! Hailwood—Honda!
I saw Agostini, in the Finnish Grand Prix at Imatra,
When Hailwood was already a legend who'd moved on
To cars. How small and pretty Ago was,
But heavily muscled like an acrobat. He smiled
And posed, enjoying his own charming looks,

While a jumpsuited mechanic pushed his silent
Racer out of the garage, and with a graceful
Sidesaddle run-and-bump started its engine.
A lion on a leash being walked in neutral
Back and forth to warm it up, it roared and roared;
Then was shut off; releasing a rather heady perfume
Of hot castor oil, as it docilely returned to the garage.

Before a race, how would Hailwood behave?
Racers get killed racing.
The roped-off crowd hushed outside the open door.
I stood in awe of Ago's ease—
In his leathers, like an animal in nature—
Inhumanly unintrospective, now smiling less
Brilliantly, but by far the brightest being in the room.

I feared finding his fear,
And looked for it,
And looked away so as not to mar the perfect.
There was an extraordinary girl there to study
Instead; and the altar piece, the lily
Painted the dried blood MV racing red,
Slender and pure—one hundred eighty miles an hour.

A lion which is a lily,
From the land of Donatello: where else could they design
Streamlined severe elegance in a toy color?
A phallus which was musical when it roared? By contrast,
Hailwood's Honda had been an unsteerable monster,
Only a genius could have won on it,
All engine and no art.

A lily that's a lion: handmade with love
By the largest helicopter manufacturer in Europe,
Whose troop carriers shielded junta and emir from harm,
And cicatriced presidents clutching
A golden ceremonial fly whisk and CIA dollars.
How storybook that a poor country boy
Should ride the Stradivarius of a count—

The aristocrat industrialist Agusta—against
The middle-class son of a nicely well-off businessman;
English; and weekly wallowing near death
On the nearly ungovernable Japanese horsepower.
A clone of Detroit, Honda Company, in going for power,
Empire-building
In peacetime displaced to motorcycle sales.

Honda raced no more. No need to to
Sell Hondas now. The empire flourished elsewhere
Than glory. I swooned in the gray even indoor air
Of a garage in Finland, as racetime neared.
Daylight blinded the doorway—the day beyond,
The crowd outside, were far away. I studied
The amazing beauty, whom Ago seemed determined to ignore.

Seated like Agostini in skintight racing leathers.
Her suit looked sweet, like Dr. Denton's on a child;
Until—as she stood up—the infant's-wear blue-innocence
Swelled violently to express
The breasts and buttocks of a totem, Magna Mater,
Overwhelming and almost ridiculous,
Venus in a racing suit,

Built big as Juno—out of place but filling up
The room, if you looked at her, which no one else did;
Though I still couldn't tell
Who she was, whose friend she was, if she was anyone's;
Whose girl, the one woman in the room.
The meaning of the enormous quiet split
Into men and woman around the motorcycle.

I thought of Sandy Moon,
Advancing toward me through the years to find me there,
Moving toward me through the years across the room
I'd rented, to hide and work,
Near Foley Square; where I wrote, and didn't write—
Through the sky-filled tall windows
Staring out for hours

At the State Supreme Court building with its steps
And columns, and the Federal Courthouse with its,
And that implacably unadorned low solid, the Department
Of Motor Vehicles. I'd leaf
Through one of my old motorcycle mags
And think of Sandy Moon—and here she was,
Naked and without a word walking slowly toward me.

Women have won. The theme is
Only for a cello, is the lurking glow
Pooled in the folds of a rich velvet, darkly phosphorescent.
Summer thunder rumbled over Brooklyn, a far-off sadness.
Naked power and a mane of glory
Shall inherit the earth. Outside the garage,
The engine caught and roared—time to go.

FUCKING

I wake because the phone is really ringing.
A singsong West Indian voice
In the dark, possibly a man's,
Blandly says, "Good morning, Mr. Seidel;
How are you feeling, God?"
And hangs up after my silence.

This is New York—
Some mornings five women call within a half hour.

In a restaurant, a woman I had just met, a Swede,
Three inches taller
Than I was among other things, and immensely
Impassive, cold,
Started to groan, very softly and husky voiced.
She said,
"You have utter control over me, and you know it.
I can't do anything about it."
I had been asking her about her job.

One can spend a lifetime trying to believe
These things.

I think of A.,
Before she became Lady Q.,
Of her lovely voice, and her lovely name.
What an extraordinary new one she took
With her marriage vows,
Even as titles go, extra fictitious. And ah—
And years later, at her request, paying a call on the husband

To ask if I could take her out
Once more, once, m'lord, for auld lang syne. She still wanted
To run away;
And had,
Our snowed-in week in the Chelsea
Years before.
How had her plane managed to land?

How will my plane manage to land?
How wilt thy plane manage to land?

Our room went out sledding for hours
And only returned when we slept,
Finally, with it still snowing, near dawn.

I can remember her sex,
And how the clitoris was set.

Now on to London where the play resumes—
The scene when I call on the husband. But first,

In Francis Bacon's queer after-hours club,
Which one went to after
An Old Compton Street Wheeler's lunch,
A gentleman at the bar, while Francis was off pissing,
Looking straight at me, shouted
"Champagne for the Norm'!"
Meaning normal, heterosexual.

The place where I stayed,
The genteel crowded gloom of Jimmy's place,
Was England—coiled in the bars of an electric fire

In Edith Grove.
Piece by piece Jimmy sold off the Georgian silver.
Three pretty working girls were his lodgers.

Walking out in one direction, you were in
Brick and brown oppidan Fulham.
Walking a few steps the other way, you heard
Augustus John's many mistresses
Twittering in the local Finch's,
And a few steps further on, in the smart restaurants,
The young grandees who still said "gels."

There was a man named Pericles Belleville,
There is a man named Pericles Belleville,
Half American.
At a very formal dinner party,
At which I met the woman I have loved the most
In my life, Belleville
Pulled out a sterling silver–plated revolver
And waved it around, pointing it at people, who smiled.
One didn't know if the thing could be fired.

That is the poem.

WHAT ONE MUST CONTEND WITH

There was a man without ability.
He talked arrogance, secretly sick at heart.
Imagine law school with his terrible stutter!—
He gagged to be smooth. But it wasn't good.
Hadn't he always planned to move on to writing?
Which of course failed, how would it not? He called
Himself a writer but it didn't work,
He chose middling friends he could rise above
But it made no difference, with no ability.

He talked grand, the terrible endearing stutter.
Batting his eyes as if it felt lovely.
He batted and winced his self-hate, like near a sneeze.
He wrote and wrote, still he could not write,
He even published, but he could not write:
The stories one story of honey and abuse—
Love and the law—he was the boy . . . de Sade
Scratching his quill raw just once to get it off.
His pen leaked in *Redbook* the preseminal drool.

He must do something, do *something*. Boy you can
Reminisce forever about Harvard,
The motorboat won't run on your perfume,
Endless warm anecdotes about past girls
Aren't a wax your cross-country skis will ride on.
He took an office just like Norman Mailer.
He married a writer just like—yes exactly.
He shaved his beard off just like—et cetera.
It is a problem in America.

You never know who's dreaming about you.
They must do *something* to try to shift the weight
They wear—painted and smiling like gold the lead!
No wonder he walked staidly. They've time to dream.
Oh hypocrites in hell dying to catch up!
Oh in etterno faticoso manto!
And if you hail one and stop—he's coming—he'll stutter,
"Costui par vivo all'atto della gola,"
"This man seems alive, by the working of his throat."

The dreaming envying third-rate writhe in America.
He sucked his pipe. He skied he fished he published.
He fucked his wife's friends. Touching himself he murmured
He was not fit to touch his wife's hem.
He dreamed of running away with his sister-in-law!
Of doing a screenplay. Him the guest on a talk show—
Wonderful—who has read and vilifies Freud!
How he'd have liked to put Freud in his place,
So really clever Freud was, but he was lies.

It was autumn. It rained. *His* lies drooped down.
It was a Year of the Pig in Vietnam,
In Vietnam our year the nth, the Nixonth,
Sometimes one wants to cut oneself in two
At the neck. The smell. The gore. To kill! There was
The child batting her head against the wall,
Beating back and forth like a gaffed fish.
There was the wife who suspected they were nothing.
There's the head face-up in the glabrous slop.

You feel for him, the man was miserable.
It's mad t-*tooh* be so ad hominem!
And *avid*, when the fellow was in Vermont,
For Southeast Asia. Was he miserable?
Another creative couple in Vermont,
The wife toasts the husband's trip to New York,
The little evening he's planning. In less than a day
He will enter my poem. He picks at her daube.
There's the head face-up in the glabrous slop.

Voilà donc quelqu'un de bien quelconque!
Ah Vermont! The artists aggregate,
A suburb of the Iowa Writers' Workshop
Except no blacks with no ability.
I am looking down at you, at you and yours,
Your stories and friends, your banal ludicrous dreams,
Dear boy, the horror, mouth uncreating,
Horror, horror, I hear it, head chopped off,
The stuttering head face-up in a pile of slop.

Just stay down there dear boy it is your home.
The unsharpened knives stuck to the wall
Magnet-bar dully. The rain let off the hush
Of a kettle that doesn't sing. Each leaf was touched,
Each leaf drooped down, a dry palm and thin wrist.
His beautifully battered sweet schoolboy satchel walked
With him out the door into scrutiny,
The ears for eyes of a bat on the wings of a dove.
Art won't forgive life, no more than life will.

ROBERT KENNEDY

I turn from Yeats to sleep, and dream of Robert Kennedy,
Assassinated ten years ago tomorrow.
Ten years ago he was alive—
Asleep and dreaming at this hour, dreaming
His wish-fulfilling dreams.
He reaches from the grave.

Shirtsleeves rolled up, a boy's brown hair, ice eyes
Softened by the suffering of others, and doomed;
Younger brother of a murdered president,
Senator and candidate for president;
Shy, compassionate and fierce
Like a figure out of Yeats;
The only politician I have loved says *You're dreaming* and says
The gun is mightier than the word.

From

These Days

(1989)

SCOTLAND

A stag lifts his nostrils to the morning
In the crosshairs of the scope of love,
And smells what the gun calls Scotland and falls.
The meat of geology raw is Scotland: Stone
Age hours of stalking, passionate aim for the heart,
Bleak dazzling weather of the bare and green.
Old men in kilts, their beards are lobster red.
Red pubic hair of virgins white as cows.
Omega under Alpha, rock hymen, fog penis—
The unshaved glow of her underarms is the sky
Of prehistory or after the sun expands.

The sun will expand a billion years from now
And burn away the mist of Caithness—till then,
There in the Thurso phone book is Robin Thurso.
But he is leaving for his other castle.
"Yes, I'm just leaving—what a pity! I can't
Remember, do you shoot?" Dukes hunt stags,
While Scotsmen hunt for jobs and emigrate,
Or else start seeing red spots on a moor
That flows to the horizon like a migraine.
Sheep dot the moor, bubblebaths of unshorn
Curls somehow red, unshepherded, unshorn.

Gone are the student mobs chanting the *Little Red
Book* of Mao at their Marxist dons.
The universities in the south woke,
Now they are going back to the land of dreams—
Tour buses clog the roads that take them there.
Gone, the rebel psychoanalysts.
Scotland trained more than its share of brilliant ones.
Pocked faces, lean as wolves, they really ran
To untrain and be famous in London, doing wild
Analysis, vegetarians brewing
Herbal tea for anorexic girls.

Let them eat haggis. The heart, lungs, and liver
Of a sheep minced with cereal and suet,
Seasoned with onions, and boiled in the sheep's stomach.
That's what the gillie eats, not venison,
Or salmon, or grouse served rare, not for the gillie
That privilege, or the other one which is
Mushed vegetables molded to resemble a steak.
Let them come to Scotland and eat blood
Pud from a food stall out in the open air,
In the square in Portree. Though there is nothing
Better in the world than a grouse cooked right.

They make a malt in Wick that tastes as smooth
As Mouton when you drink enough of it.
McEwen adored both, suffered a partial stroke,
Switched to champagne and died. A single piper
Drones a file of mourners through a moor,
The sweet prodigal being piped to his early grave.
A friend of his arriving by helicopter
Spies the procession from a mile away,
The black speck of the coffin trailing a thread,
Lost in the savage green, an ocean of thawed
Endlessness and a spermatozoon.

A vehement bullet comes from the gun of love.
On the island of Raasay across from Skye,
The dead walk with the living hand in hand
Over to Hallaig in the evening light.
Girls and boys of every generation,
MacLeans and MacLeods, as they were before they were
Mothers and clansmen, still in their innocence,
Walk beside the islanders, their descendants.
They hold their small hands up to be held by the living.
Their love is too much, the freezing shock-alive
Of rubbing alcohol that leads to sleep.

FLAME

The honey, the humming of a million bees,
In the middle of Florence pining for Paris;
The whining trembling the cars and trucks hum
Crossing the metal matting of Brooklyn Bridge
When you stand below it on the Brooklyn side—
High above you, the harp, the cathedral, the hive—
In the middle of Florence. Florence in flames.

Like waking from a fever . . . it is evening.
Fireflies breathe in the gardens on Bellosguardo.
And then the moon steps from the cypresses and
A wave of feeling breaks, phosphorescent—
Moonlight, a wave hushing on a beach.
In the dark, a flame goes out. And then
The afterimage of a flame goes out.

OUR GODS

Older than us, but not by that much, men
Just old enough to be uncircumcised,
Episcopalians from the Golden Age
Of schools who loved to lose gracefully and lead—
Always there before us like a mirage,
Until we tried to get closer, when they vanished,
Always there until they disappeared.

They were the last of a race, that was their cover—
The baggy tweeds. Exposed in the Racquet Club
Dressing room, they were invisible,
Present purely in outline like the head
And torso targets at the police firing
Range, hairless bodies and full heads of hair,
Painted neatly combed, of the last WASPs.

They walked like boys, talked like their grandfathers—
Public servants in secret, and the last
Generation of men to prefer baths.
These were the CIA boys with EYES
ONLY clearance and profiles like arrowheads.
A fireside frost bloomed on the silver martini
Shaker the magic evenings they could be home.

They were never home, even when they were there.
Public servants in secret are not servants,
Either. They were our gods working all night
To make Achilles' beard fall out and prop up
The House of Priam, who by just pointing sent
A shark fin gliding down a corridor,
Almost transparent, like a watermark.

THAT FALL

The body on the bed is made of china,
Shiny china vagina and pubic hair.
The glassy smoothness of a woman's body!
I stand outside the open door and stare.

I watch the shark glide by . . . it comes and goes—
Must constantly keep moving or it will drown.
The mouth slit in the formless fetal nose
Gives it that empty look—it looks unborn;

It comes into the room up to the bed
Just like a dog. The smell of burning leaves,
Rose bittersweetness rising from the red,
Is what I see. I must be twelve. That fall.

A DIMPLED CLOUD

Cold drool on his chin, warm drool in his lap, a sigh,
The bitterness of too many cigarettes
On his breath: portrait of the autist
Asleep in the arms of his armchair, age thirteen,
Dizzily starting to wake just as the sun
Is setting. The room is already dark while outside
Rosewater streams from a broken yolk of blood.

All he has to do to sleep is open
A book; but the wet dream is new, as if
The pressure of *De bello Gallico*
And Willa Cather face down on his fly,
Spread wide, one clasping the other from behind,
Had added confusion to confusion, like looking
For your glasses with your glasses on.

A mystically clear, unknowing trance of being . . .
And then you feel them—like that, his first wet dream
Seated in a chair, though not his first.
Mr. Hobbs, the Latin master with
A Roman nose he's always blowing, who keeps
His gooey handkerchief tucked in his jacket sleeve,
Pulls his hanky out, and fades away.

French, English, math, history: masters one
By one arrive, start to do what they do
In life, some oddity, some thing they do,
Then vanish. The darkness of the room grows brighter
The darker it gets outside, because of the moonlight.
O adolescence! darkness of a hole
The silver moonlight fills to overflowing!

If only he could be von Schrader or
Deloges, a beautiful athlete or a complete
Shit. God, von Schrader lazily shagging flies,
The beautiful flat trajectory of his throw.
Instead of seeking power, being it!
Tomorrow Deloges will lead the school in prayer,
Not that the autist would want to take his place.

Naked boys are yelling and snapping wet towels
At each other in the locker room,
Like a big swordfighting scene from *The Three Musketeers*,
Parry and thrust, roars of laughter and rage,
Lush Turkish steam billowing from the showers.
The showers hiss, the air is silver fox.
Hot breath, flashes of swords, the ravishing fur!—

Swashbuckling boys brandishing their towels!
Depression, aggression, elation—and acne cream—
The ecosystem of a boy his age.
He combs his wet hair straight, he hates his curls,
He checks his pimples. Only the biggest ones show,
Or rather the ointment on them caked like mud,
Supposedly skin-color, invisible; dabs

Of peanut butter that have dried to fossils,
That even a shower won't wash away, like flaws
Of character expressed by their concealment—
Secrets holding up signs—O adolescence!
O silence not really hidden by the words,
Which are not true, the words, the words, the words—
Unless you scrub, will not wash away.

But how sweetly they strive to outreach these shortcomings,
These boys who call each other by their last names,
Copying older boys and masters—it's why
He isn't wearing his glasses, though he can't see.
That fiend Deloges notices but says nothing.
Butting rams, each looks at the other sincerely,
And doesn't look away, blue eyes that lie.

He follows his astigmatism toward
The schoolbuses lined up to take everyone home,
But which are empty still, which have that smiling,
Sweet-natured blur of the retarded, oafs
In clothes too small, too wrong, too red and white,
And *painfully* eager to please a sadist so cruel
He wouldn't even hurt a masochist.

The sadistic eye of the autist shapes the world
Into a sort of, call it innocence,
Ready to be wronged, ready to
Be tortured into power and beauty, into
Words his phonographic memory
Will store on silence like particles of oil
On water—the rainbow of polarity

Which made this poem. I put my glasses on,
And shut my eyes. O adolescence, sing!
All the bus windows are open because it's warm.
I blindly face a breeze almost too sweet
To bear. I hear a hazy drone and float—
A dimpled cloud—above the poor white and poorer
Black neighborhoods which surround the small airfield.

THE BLUE-EYED DOE

I look at Broadway in the bitter cold,
The center strip benches empty like today,
And see St. Louis. I am often old
Enough to leave my childhood, but I stay.

A winter sky as total as repression
Above a street the color of the sky;
A sky the same gray as a deep depression;
A boulevard the color of a sigh:

Where Waterman and Union met was the
Apartment building I'm regressing to.
My key is in the door; I am the key;
I'm opening the door. I think it's true

Childhood is your mother even if
Your mother is in hospitals for years
And then lobotomized, like mine. A whiff
Of her perfume; behind her veil, her tears.

She wasn't crying anymore. Oh try.
No afterward she wasn't anymore.
But yes she will, she is. Oh try to cry.
I'm here—right now I'm walking through the door.

The pond was quite wide, but the happy dog
Swam back and forth called by the boy, then by
His sister on the other side, a log
Of love putt-putting back and forth from fry

To freeze, from freeze to fry, a normal pair
Of the extremes of normal, on and on.
The dog was getting tired; the children stare—
Their childhood's over. Everyone is gone,

Forest Park's deserted; still they call.
It's very cold. Soprano puffs of breath,
Small voices calling in the dusk is all
We ever are, pale speech balloons. One death,

Two ghosts . . . white children playing in a park
At dusk forever—but we must get home.
The mica sidewalk sparkles in the dark
And starts to freeze—or fry—and turns to foam.

At once the streetlights in the park go on.
Gas hisses from the trees—but it's the wind.
The real world vanishes behind the fawn
That leaps to safety while the doe is skinned.

The statue of Saint Louis on Art Hill,
In front of the museum, turns into
A blue-eyed doe. Next it will breathe. Soon will
Be sighing, dripping tears as thick as glue.

Stags do that when the hunt has cornered them.
The horn is blown. Bah-ooo. Her mind a doe
Which will be crying soon at bay. The stem
Between the autumn leaf and branch lets go.

My mother suddenly began to sob.
If only she could do that now. Oh try.
I feel the lock unlock. Now try the knob.
Sobbed uncontrollably. Oh try to cry.

How easily I can erase an error,
The typos my recalling this will cause,
But no correcting key erases terror.
One ambulance attendant flashed his claws,

The other plunged the needle in. They squeeze
The plunger down, the brainwash out. Bah-ooo.
Calm deepened in her slowly. There, they ease
Her to her feet. White Goddess, blond, eyes blue—

Even from two rooms away I see
The blue, if that is possible! Bright white
Of the attendants; and the mystery
And calm of the madonna; and my fright.

I flee, but to a mirror. In it, they
Are rooms behind me in our entrance hall
About to leave—the image that will stay
With me. My future was behind me. All

The future is a mirror in which they
Are still behind me in the entrance hall,
About to leave—and if I look away
She'll vanish. Once upon a time, a fall

So long ago that they were burning leaves,
Which wasn't yet against the law, I looked
Away. I watched the slowly flowing sleeves
Of smoke, the blood-raw leaf piles being cooked,

Sweet-smelling scenes of mellow preparation
Around a bloodstained altar, but instead
Of human sacrifice, a separation.
My blue-eyed doe! The severed blue-eyed head!

The windows were wide-open through which I
Could flee to nowhere—nowhere meaning how
The past is portable, and therefore why
The future of the past was always now

A treeless Art Hill gleaming in the snow,
The statue of Saint Louis at the top
On horseback, blessing everything below,
Tobogganing the bald pate into slop.

Warm sun, blue sky; blond hair, blue eyes; of course
They'll shave her head for the lobotomy,
They'll cut her brain, they'll kill her at the source.
When she's wheeled out, blue eyes are all I see.

The bandages—down to her eyes—give her
A turbaned twenties look, but I'm confused.
There were no bandages. I saw a blur.
They didn't touch a hair—but I'm confused.

I breathe mist on the mirror . . . I am here—
Blond hair I pray will darken till it does,
Blue eyes that will need glasses in a year—
I'm here and disappear, the boy I was . . .

The son who lifts his sword above Art Hill;
Who holds it almost like a dagger but
In blessing, handle up, and not to kill;
Who holds it by the blade that cannot cut.

From

My Tokyo

(1993)

HAIR IN A NET

If you're a woman turning fifty,
You're a woman who feels cheated.
This message now will be repeated.

The bittersweetness known as Jesus
Was not some nice man saying he is
Not quite a feminist and not quite not one.

Every man's a rapist until he's done.
The bitch relieves the dog. The wound, the gun.
The Sermon on the Mount, the Son.

Was it better back in Peapack
Riding over hills to hounds,
Your consciousness not yet raised?

At Foxcroft, under Miss Charlotte,
Polishing your boots till they were bittersweet,
The fields were a girl's cantata.

Doing the rumba at the regatta,
Plato in Greek, amphetamines your stallion, were your alma mater,
And the Metropolitan, and the Modern . . . and then S/M.

Oh, the tiny furs and the red stench of the fox
Of all those white girls taking cold showers
And then lining up to jump

Hair in a net in a hat over perfectly maintained fences.
Everything male is a rapist, certainly God,
Except for Henry James.

At the Institute for Advanced Study,
Which your father helped organize,
Your father made lives,

Scientists he saved from the Nazis,
Putting his face on the cover of *Time*,
Or was that for his part in building the Atom Bomb?

And otherwise—the man made gushers in Texas rise.
He macadamized the roads of Greece.
His sword was terrible and swift.

He strode up the hill in the heat.
He dove into the ice-cold pool and burst
Instantly into death like a flame.

THE RITZ, PARIS

A slight thinness of the ankles;
The changed shape of the calf;
A place the thigh curves in
Where it didn't used to; and when he turns
A mirror catches him by surprise
With an old man's buttocks.

GLORY

Herbert Brownell was the attorney general.
Ezra Pound was reciting some Provençal. I was seventeen
Every terrifying hungover sunrise that fall.
Thanksgiving weekend 1953 I made my pilgrimage to Pound,
Who said, Kike-sucking Pusey will destroy Harvard unless you save it.
I persuaded him two words in his translation of Confucius should change.

His pal Achilles Fang led me to the empty attic of the Yenching Institute,
In the vast gloom arranged two metal folding chairs
Under the one lightbulb hanging from the ceiling,
And hating me, knee to knee,
Unsmilingly asked, What do you know?
Pound sent a message to MacLeish. Archie, wake up.

United States of America v. Ezra Pound.
My song will seek and detonate your heat.
Pound reciting with his eyes closed filled the alcove with glory.
My art will find and detonate your heart.
I was a freshman and everywhere in Washington, D.C.
I walked, I dreamed.

SONNET

The suffering in the sunlight and the smell.
And the bellowing and men weeping and screaming.
And the horses wandering aimlessly and the heat.
The living and the dead mixed, bleeding on one another.
A palm with two fingers left attached
Lying on the ground next to the hindquarters of a horse.
A dying man literally without a face
Pointed at where his face had been.
He did this without a sound.
The forty thousand dead and wounded stretched for miles
In every direction from the tower.
Not a cloud in the sky all day, the sunlight of hell.
Bodies swelled and split, erupting their insides
Like sausages on the fire.

BURKINA FASO

The first is take the innards out when you
Do Ouagadougou. Clean with a grenade.
Thus Captain Compaoré's kitchen made
From Clément Ouedraogo human stew.

The one man who might help them disappears
And reappears in bowls. You eat or are
The eaten here. French-speaking, Muslim tar
That once sold slaves and blames the French, in tears.

POL POT

Dawn. Leni Riefenstahl
And her cameras slowly inflate the immense Nuremberg Rally.
The Colorado looks up in awe at the Grand Canyon
It has made. Hitler.

European clouds. 1934. Empty
Thought-balloons high above Lascaux
Without a thought inside. The Führer
Is ice that's fire, physically small.

They all were. Stalin.
Trotsky's little glasses
Disappear behind a cloud
From which he won't emerge alive.

The small plane carrying
The Grail to Nuremberg got Wagnerian clouds
To fly through, enormous, enormous. Mine eyes have seen the glory, it
Taxis to a stop. The cabin door swings open.

Leni schussed from motion pictures
To still photography after the war. From the Aryan ideal, climbed out
In Africa to shoot the wild shy people of Kau,
Small heads, tall, the most beautiful animals in the world.

Artistically mounted them into ideal
Riefenstahl. Riefenstahl! Riefenstahl! Riefenstahl! Really,
From blonds in black-and-white to blacks in color.
Now Pol Pot came to power.

Now in London Sylvia Plath
Nailed one foot to the floor;
And with the other walked
And walked and walked through the terrible blood.

STROKE

The instrument is priceless.
You can't believe it happened.
The restoration flawless.
The voice is almost human.
The sound is almost painful.
The voice is almost human.
I close my eyes to hear it.
The restoration flawless.
The beauty is inhuman.
The terrifying journey.
O strange new final music.
The strange new place I've gone to.
The blinding light is music.
The starless warm night blinding.
The odor of a musk rose
Presents itself as secrets.
Paralysis can't stop them.
The afterburners kick in.
The visitors are going.
I dreamed that I was sleeping.
Physiatry can't say it.
I can't believe it happened.
A handshake is the human
Condition of bereavement.
A thixotropic sol is
A shaken-up false body.
I know another meaning.
A life was last seen living.
A life was last seen leaving.
The summit of Mount Sinai,

The top of their new tower,
The stark New North Pavilion,
Looks out on New York City,
The miles of aspiration,
The lonely devastation.
I listen to the music
Nine years before 2000.

.

MY TOKYO

Moshi-moshi. (Hello.)
Money is being made.
Money was being made.
Make more make more make more consumer goods.

But the shelves were empty.
The snow was deep.
At Lenin's Tomb the Honor Guard
Stood there actually asleep.

Red Square was white.
Snow was falling dreamily on Beijing.
This was global warming.
Twenty-four hours passed and it was still snowing.

In New York the homeless
Reify the rich.
The homeless in the streets.
The car alarms go off.

The cherry blossoms burst
Into Imperial bloom. The handheld fax machine has something
Coming in. This spring our Western eyes are starting to slant.
They caution you composites can't.

O O O Ochanomizu,
You are my station.
The polished businessman warrior bowed
Cool as a mountain forest of pine.

And the adolescent schoolgirls like clouds of butterflies
On the subway in their black school uniforms
At all hours of the day going somewhere,
Daughters of the Rising Sun.

New York is an electrical fire.
People are trapped on the top floor, smoking
With high-rise desire
And becoming Calcutta.

Tokyo is low
And manic as a hive.
For the middle of the night they have silent jackhammers.
Elizabethan London with the sound off. Racially pure with no poor.

Mishima himself designed the stark far-out uniform
His private army wore, madly haute couture. He stabbed the blade in wrong
And was still alive while his aide tried in vain
To cut his head off as required.

Moshi-moshi I can't hear you. I'm going blind.
Don't let me abandon you, you're all I have.
Hello, hello. My Tokyo, hello.
Hang up and I'll call you back.

You say to the recyclable person of your dreams *Je t'aime*,
And the voice recognition system,
Housed in a heart made from seaweed,
Murmurs in Japanese *Moi aussi*.

From

Going Fast

(1998)

MIDNIGHT

God begins. The universe will soon.
The intensity of the baseball bat
Meets the ball. Is the fireball
When he speaks and then in the silence
The cobra head rises regally and turns to look at you.
The angel burns through the air.
The flower turns to look.

The cover of the book opens on its own.
You do not want to see what is on this page.
It looks up at you,
Only it is a mirror you are looking into.
The truth is there, and all around the truth fire
Makes a frame.
Listen. An angel. These sounds you hear are his.

A dog is barking in a field.
A car starts in the parking lot on the other side.
The ocean heaves back and forth three blocks away.
The fire in the wood stove eases
The inflamed cast-iron door
Open, steps out into the room across the freezing floor
To your perfumed bed where as it happens you kneel and pray.

PRAYER

But we are someone else. We're born that way.
The other one we are lives in a distant city.
People are walking down a street.
They pop umbrellas open when it starts to rain.
Some stand under an apartment building awning.
A doorman dashes out into the spring shower for
A taxi with its off-duty light on that hisses right past.
The daffodils are out on the avenue center strip.
The yellow cabs are yellow as the daffodils.
One exhausted driver, at the end of his ten-hour shift headed in,
Stops for the other one
We are who hides among the poor
And looks like the homeless out on the wet street corner.
Dear friend, get in.
I will take you where you're going for free.
Only a child's Crayola
Could color a taxi cab this yellow
In a distant city full of yellow flowers.

THE NIGHT SKY

At night, when she is fast asleep,
The comet, which appears not to move at all,
Crosses the sky above her bed,
But stays there looking down.

She rises from her sleeping body.
Her body stays behind asleep.
She climbs the lowered ladder.
She enters through the opened hatch.

Inside is everyone.
Everyone is there.
Someone smiling is made of silk.
Someone else was made with milk.

Her mother still alive.
Her brothers and sisters and father
And aunts and uncles and grandparents
And husband never died.

Hold the glass with both hands,
My darling, that way you won't spill.
On her little dress, her cloth yellow star
Comet travels through space.

THE STARS ABOVE THE EMPTY QUARTER

A cat has caught a mouse and is playing

At letting it go is the sun

Over the desert letting the traveler reach the oasis.

The sink vomits all over itself

Is the sand boiling down from the blond sky in a storm.

A pre-Islamic Golden Ode lists

The hundred qualities of a camel.

Suavity, power, the beauty of its eyes.

Its horn, its tires, its perfect bumpers, its perfect fenders.

The way it turns left, the way it turns right.

The great poet Labīd sings

His Song of Songs about the one he loves.

How long it can go without water and without God.

Sings the nomad life of hardship, calls it ease.

He stares at the far-off stars.

He mounts the kneeling camel at dawn.

He lowers himself and rises.

I sing above the sand under the sun.

CONTENTS UNDER PRESSURE

His space suit is his respirator breathing him
From its own limited supply of oxygen.
The hand-controlled jet nozzles squirted him away
On a space walk in short bursts that have gone haywire.
But will stop when there is no fuel seconds from now. Now.
The long tether back to the mother spaceship sticks
Straight out from his back weightlessly
In the zero gravity of space.
It has sheared off at the other end.
Absolutely nothing can be done.
The spacecraft is under orders not to try and to return and does.
He urinates and defecates
And looks out at the universe.
He is looking out at it through his helmet mask.

AT GRACIE MANSION

I like motorcycles, the city, the telephone.
TV but not to watch, just to turn it on.
The women and their legs, the movies and the streets.
At dawn when it's so hot the sky is almost red.
The smell of both the rivers is the underworld exhumed.

I remember the vanished days of the great steakhouses.
Before the miniaturization in electronics.
When Robert Wagner was mayor and men ate meat.
I like air-conditioning, leather booths, linen,
Heat, Milan, Thomas Jefferson.

The woman got red in the face touching her girlfriend live
On one of the cable public access shows you do yourself.
Part of the redundancy built into servo systems
That can fail was when she started to spank the girl.
I took her heat straight to my heart.

I never watch TV.
But sometimes late at night. My friend
The junior senator from Nebraska, the only
Medal of Honor winner in Congress, reads Mandelstam,
Reads Joseph Roth. What happens next?

When Wagner's first wife died of cancer,
And Bennett Cerf died of cancer,
Phyllis Cerf and Bob got married—and then Bob died of cancer.
Bobby, Jr., restored by Giuliani, dropped dead on a plane to L.A.
At the age of forty-nine.

How's that again?
Bobby died suddenly in a hotel room in San Antonio.
Bennett expired from Parkinson's.
It ought to matter what battlefield you died on.
A deputy mayor under Koch and the founder of Random House.

I like it when the long line of headlights on behind the hearse
Is stuck in backed-up traffic on the Drive.
A tug tows a barge slowly by
The closed smoked-glass windows of the limousines.
I read Olmsted. I kiss the parks commissioner.

I like anything worth dying for.
I like the brave. I like the Type A personality which is hot.
I like the hideous embarrassment of Nelson Rockefeller
Dying inside somebody young.
He had an attack heart.

I watch a floater in my eye cross Jimmy Walker on the wall.
I like the bead curtains of hot rain outside on the street.
I hold a "see-through on a stem," an ice-cold martini.
Take the heat in your hand. It is cold.
Take the heat. Drink.

MOOD INDIGO

One was blacker.
The other one was frightened.
They cut the phone wires.
They used my neckties.
They had me on my stomach.
They tied a hangman's noose around my neck
And stretched the rope of neckties down my back
To my wrists and ankles.
The slightest movement choked me.
He grabbed a carving knife I had
And stabbed me in the temple over and over,
While his partner looked on in horror,
And never even broke the skin,
A technique used in Vietnam.
He find the biggest knife he can
An stab this white boy pretty good
An never even break the skin,
A torture used in Vietnam.
A war there is
And stuck it in a sideburn hard
And didn't even scratch the surface.

SPRING

I want to date-rape life. I kiss the cactus spines.
Running a fever in the cold keeps me alive.
My twin, the garbage truck seducing Key Food, whines
And dines and crushes, just like me, and wants to drive.
I want to drive into a drive-in bank and kiss
And kill you, life. Sag Harbor, I'm your lover. I'm
Yours, Sagaponack, too. This shark of bliss
I input generates a desert slick as slime.

DUNE ROAD, SOUTHAMPTON

The murderer has been injecting her remorselessly
With succinylcholine, which he mixes in her daily insulin.
She's too weak to give herself her shots. By the time she has figured it out,
She is helpless.

She can't move any part of her face.
She can't write a note.
She can't speak
To say she hasn't had a stroke.

It's terrifying that she's aware
That something terrible is being done to her.
One day he ups the dose. And gets scared.
She has to be rushed to the local hospital and intubated.

They know at the hospital who she is,
One of the richest women in the world.
The murderer hands the attending a faked M.R.I.
It flaunts the name of a world authority. Showing she has had a stroke.

The neurologist on call introduces herself to the murderer and concurs.
Locked-in syndrome, just about the worst.
Alive, with staring eyes.
The mind is unaffected.

And with the patient looking on expressionlessly,
Screaming don't let him take me home, without a sign or sound,
The doctor tells the murderer he can take her home,
If that's their wish.

Their little beach house has forty rooms.

Her elevator is carved mahogany.

The Great Gatsby swimming pool upstairs is kept full and never used.

Her tower bedroom flies out over the winter ocean, spreading its wings.

Mother, you're going to die,

He tells her, once they're alone.

You have the right to remain silent.

I'm making a joke.

I'll read you your rights.

He takes a syringe.

A woman has the right to bare arms. I particularly like them bare.

I might as well be talking to cement.

IN MEMORIAM

Great-grandson of George Boole as in Boolean algebra.
First in his class at Cambridge till he received an inheritance.
Spent it all brilliantly in a flash flood of champagne.
Loved girls and genius. Loved Lord Rothschild his friend.

After a gentleman's Third fled to Paris.
Out of money but life was sweet.
Whisky and style and car-running across borders.
Imprisoned in Spain terrifying.

Meanwhile his father with whom he'd almost had a rapprochement died.
Rothschild visited him in prison once.
How can a boy renounce himself? He began.
But years later he was wonderfully still the same.

Letting rooms to pretty lodgers.
Selling off the Georgian silver piece by piece.
Fired as the engineering consultant for refusing to lie to England.
British Steel tried hard to ruin him but he won.

Stuttered and lisped and wouldn't look you in the eye
In a lofty gwandly Edwardian way.
Jimmy, in America it'll make you seem shifty.
Laughter and delight and he looks you in the eye for a second.

ANYONE WITH THE WISH

The lagoon of the biggest atoll in the world,
So wide across you can't see the other shore,
Is soft as dew.
Water is love
In Rangiroa.

Fish move away from you without fear,
Like buffalo on the plains before they disappeared.
The boat far above you on the surface waits,
The pale hull,
The motor as gonads.

You haven't come here only for the shark show.
Their fixed smiles glide.
Their blank eyes go along for the ride.
They bury their face in life explosively,
And shake their head back and forth to tear some off.

Every day a guide sets out a bait
So anyone with the wish can swim with the sharks,
And circle the meat,
And feel close to the teeth.
Sharks swim in the love.

A GALLOP TO FAREWELL

Three unrelated establishments named Caraceni in Milan
On streets not far apart make custom suits for men.
They are the best,
Autistically isolated in the pure,
Some might say in the pure
Pursuit of gracefully clothing manure.
Superb, discreet, threading their way to God,
The suits curve with beauty and precision,
Perfection on the order of Huntsman in Savile Row
And their jacket cutter, Mr. Hall.

The attitude to take to shoes is there is Lobb.
The one in Paris, not the one in London.
No one has surpassed
The late George Cleverley's lasts,
The angle in of the heel, the slightly squared-off toe, the line,
Though Suire at Lobb is getting there.
His shoes fit like paradise by the third pair.
Like they were Eve. The well-dressed man,
The vein of gold that seems inexhaustible,
Is a sunstream of urine on its way to the toilet bowl.

A rich American sadist had handcuffs made at Hermès
To torture with beauty the duchesse d'Uzès.
A cow looking at the understated elegance would know
Simplicity as calm as this was art.
A briefcase from Hermès
Is ravishing and stark.
Flawless leather luxury made for horses out of cows
Is what the horsy cows grazing daily in the Faubourg St-Honoré store
Want to buy. Tour group cows in a feeding frenzy
Devour everything like locusts.

There are travelers who prefer the British Concorde to the French
For the interior in beige and gray.
Hermès has created a carry-on in water buffalo
For them called the Gallop.
Their seat is in the first cabin.
Three kinds of Caraceni suits chose the aisle.
The most underrated pleasure in the world is the takeoff
Of the Concorde and putting off the crash
Of the world's most beautiful old supersonic plane, with no survivors,
In an explosion of champagne.

A VAMPIRE IN THE AGE OF AIDS

He moves carefully away from the extremely small pieces
Of human beings spread around for miles, still in his leather seat.
He looks like a hunchback walking in the Concorde chair,
Bent over, strapped in, eyes on the ground
To avoid stepping on the soft.
He will use his influence to get
The cockpit voice recorder when it is recovered copied.
He loves the pilot in the last ninety seconds'
Matter-of-factness turning into weeping screams,
Undead in the double-breasted red velvet smoking jacket Huntsman made.

ANOTHER MUSE

Another muse appeared, but dressed in black,
Which turned to skin the minute the light was out.
He had become a front without a back.
Arousal was a desert with a spout.

A string of women like a string of fish
Kept dangling in the water to keep them alive.
Washed down with Lynch-Bages to assuage the anguish
Of eating red meat during a muff dive.

One woman, then another, then another.
Drops of dew dropped into a flat green ocean.
They leaked purity and freshness, and mother.
The glass eye of each dewdrop magnified his lack of emotion.

You get a visa and some shots and buy
Provisions for the Amazon and fly
Instead to Africa and tell them I
Will always be your friend and then you try.

He was too busy musing to unchain them,
The women on a string inside the slave pen.
Feminists in nylons in his brain stem.
Escaped slaves recaptured. They crave men.

Women with shaved legs. Women in bondage.
Come out of the closet in their leg irons.
Hooded and gagged and garter-belted Lynch-Bages.
He hears the distant screaming of the sirens.

He lifts his glass. He bows. Testosterone,
The aviation fuel that gives him wings,
Drinks to the gods. His kamikaze starts its flight from his zone
For her zone. Redlined, on full honk, he sings.

SPIN

A dog named Spinach died today.
In her arms he died away.
Injected with what killed him.
Love is a cup that spilled him.
Spilled all the Spin that filled him.
Sunlight sealed and sent.
Received and spent.
Smiled and went.

EISENHOWER YEARS

Suddenly I had to eat
A slowly writhing worm
A woman warmed on a flat stone in a jungle clearing
Or starve. I had to charm a Nazi waving a Luger
Who could help me escape from a jungle river port town or die.

I had to survive not being allowed to sit down,
For ten hours, in a Mexico City
Jail, accused of manslaughter because
My cab driver in the early morning rush hour
Had killed a pedestrian and jumped out and run.

The prostitute even younger than I was that
I had spent the night with had been
So shy I had gone home with her to meet her parents
When she asked. In the Waikiki Club
Where she worked, I'd faced her machete-faced pimp wielding a knife.

At the Mayan Temple of the Moon, "that" instead of "whom,"
Which the explorer Richard Halliburton
Has written everyone must climb on a night of the full moon
At midnight who wants to say he or she has lived,
The guard dog woke the guard up.

I heard the lyrical barking from the top.
I saw the wink of the rifle barrel far below in the moonlight and hit
The deck like a commando on the ramp along the outside of the pyramid to hide
When at last I looked up Orson Welles stood there, doe-eyed sombrero silence
Expecting a bribe. I walked with him all innocence down the ramp.

I walked past him out the gate and he fired.
I felt invulnerable, without feelings, without pores.
A week after I got back home to St. Louis I fainted
At the wheel of a car just after I had dropped off a friend,
And for four months in the hospital with a tropical disease I nearly died.

Suddenly in the jungle there was an American professor named Bud Bivins
Who had fled from Texas to avoid the coming nuclear war.
The Nazi found passage for us both on a tramp steamer which ran
Into a violent storm in the Gulf not long after Bivins had gone mad
And taken to pacing the deck all night after the cook had demanded

On the captain's behalf that we pay him more, on top of what
We'd already paid, or swim, with his butcher knife pointing to a thin line
Of green at the horizon, the distant jungle shore.
The captain would be delighted to let us off immediately if we wished.
No one saw Bivins when we reached port.

In the middle of the night a huge wave hit
The rotten boatload of tarantulas and bananas, slam-dunking us under.
The cook and all the others, including our captain,
Kneeled at the rail holding on, loudly praying, so who was at the wheel?
Bivins was last spied on the deck. I was sixteen.

VERMONT

The attitude of green to blue is love.
And so the day just floats itself away.
The stench of green, the drench of green, above
The ripples of sweet swimming in a bay
Of just-mowed green, intoxicates the house.
The meadow goddess squeaking like a mouse
Is stoned, inhales the grass, adores the sky.
The nostrils feed the gods until the eye
Can almost see the perfume pour the blue.
A Botticelli ladled from a well,
Your life is anything you want it to—
And loves you more than it can show or tell.

RACINE

When civilization was European,
I knew every beautiful woman
In the Grand Hôtel et de Milan,
Which the Milanese called "The Millin,"
Where Verdi died, two blocks from La Scala,
And lived in every one of them
Twenty-some years ago while a motorcycle was being made
For me by the MV Agusta
Racing Department in Cascina Costa,
The best mechanics in the world
Moonlighting for me after racing hours.
One of the "Millin" women raced cars, a raving beauty.
She owned two Morandis, had met Montale.
She recited verses from the Koran
Over champagne in the salon and was only eighteen
And was too good to be true.
She smilingly recited Leopardi in Hebrew.
The most elegant thing in life is an Italian Jew.
The most astonishing thing in life to be is an Italian Jew.
It helps if you can be from Milan, too.
She knew every *tirade* in Racine
And was only eighteen.
They thought she was making a scene
When she started declaiming Racine.
Thunderbolts in the bar.
With the burning smell of Auschwitz in my ear.
With the gas hissing from the ceiling.
Racine raved on racing tires at the limit of adhesion.
With the gas hissing from the showers.
I remember the glamorous etching on the postcard

The hotel continued to reprint from the original 1942 plate.

The fantasy hotel and street

Had the haughty perfect ease of haute couture,

Chanel in stone. A tiny tailored doorman

Stood as in an architectural drawing in front of the façade and streamlined

Cars passed by.

The cars looked as if they had their headlights on in the rain,

In the suave, grave

Milanese sunshine.

MILAN

This is Via Gesù.
Stone without a tree.
This is the good life.
Puritan elegance.
Severe but plentiful.
Big breasts in a business suit.
Between Via Monte Napoleone and Via della Spiga.

I draw
The bowstring of Cupid's bow,
Too powerful for anything but love to pull.

Oh the sudden green gardens glimpsed through gates and the stark
Deliciously expensive shops.
I let the pocket knives at Lorenzi,
Each a priceless jewel,
Gods of blades and hinges,
Make me late for a fitting at Caraceni.

Oh Milan, I feel myself being pulled back
To the past and released.
I hiss like an arrow
Through the air,
On my way from here to there.
I am a man I used to know.
I am the arrow and the bow.
I am a reincarnation, but
I give birth to the man
I grew out of.
I follow him down a street
Into a restaurant I don't remember
And sit and eat.

A Ducati 916 stabs through the blur.
Massimo Tamburini designed this miracle
Which ought to be in the Museum of Modern Art.
The Stradivarius
Of motorcycles lights up Via Borgospesso
As it flashes by, dumbfoundingly small.
Donatello by way of Brancusi, smoothed simplicity.
One hundred sixty-four miles an hour.
The Ducati 916 is a nightingale.
It sings to me more sweetly than Cole Porter.
Slender as a girl, aerodynamically clean.
Sudden as a shark.

The president of Cagiva Motorcycles,
Mr. Claudio Castiglioni, lifts off in his helicopter
From his ecologically sound factory by a lake.
Cagiva in Varese owns Ducati in Bologna,
Where he lands.
His instructions are Confucian:
Don't stint.

Combine a far-seeing industrialist.
With an Islamic fundamentalist.
With an Italian premier who doesn't take bribes.
With a pharmaceuticals CEO who loves to spread disease.
Put them on a 916.

And you get Fred Seidel.

A PRETTY GIRL

Umber, somber, brick Bologna.
They could use some Miami Jews
In this city of sensible shoes.

In the city of Morandi,
The painter of the silence
Of groups of empty bottles,
Arcades of demure
Men dressed in brown pneumonia
Look for women in the fog.

Bare, thick, spare, pure,
Umber, somber, brick Bologna.
This year's fashion color is manure,
According to the windows
Of fogged-in manikins
In Piazza Cavour.
Reeking of allure,
Arcades of demure
Young women dressed in odorless brown pneumonia
Give off clouds of smoke,
Dry ice in the fog.

Bare, thick, spare, pure:
Shaved heads reading books flick
Their cigarettes away and cover their mouths with their scarfs,
Leaned against the radical Medical School,
Punks with stethoscopes, horoscopes.
They listen to the heart with the heart,
Students in the medieval streets.

Their tangerine fingernails heal
The Emergency Room in gloves
Till dawn, and still come out eager to Day-Glo Bologna.
The tangerine tirelessly sheds disposable latex
Gloves until the day glows.
Emergency path lighting
On the airplane floor has led me to the exits
Through the cold and the fog.

Follow the tangerine path through the dark and the smoke.
Beneath the unisex jeans
Is cunnus soft as shatoosh.

The Communist mayor who underwrites the Morandi Museum
Takes a right-wing industrialist through the silence.

And the Ducati motorcycle factory
In Via Cavalieri Ducati breathes to life
Another piece of sculpture that goes fast.
Art and engineering meet and make
A brain wave
Of beauty suitable to ride.

The advice of my physician
Is, turn sixty.

I limit lovemaking to one position,
Mounted on a Ducati, monoposto:
Equivalent to warm sand as white as snow,
And skin as brown as brandy,
And swimming in the blue of faraway.

A well-dressed man is lying on a bed
With Leopardi in his arms.
The fog outside the window is Bologna.
He does the dead man's float
Next to the sleek hull of the sloop *A Pretty Girl*,
Stuck in a sheet of glue
Which extends for a hundred miles
Without a sip of wind,
Under a sky.
The blue is infinite.
He can see three miles down.
He free-floats in glass in his body temperature.
He does not know yet that he has dived in
Forgetting to let the ladder down,
And he does not know
He cannot climb back up.
There are no handholds.
The sloping sides are smooth.
The deck too high.
She heads for the horizon under full sail
In his flash hallucination. You never
Leave no one onboard,
But he does not know yet what has happened since
A Pretty Girl is not going anywhere.
The sailboat pond in Central Park
Is where a boy's days were a breeze.
He does the dead man's float
Next to the motionless boat,
But in art there is no hope.
Art is dope.

The fog glows,
Tangerine toward sundown.

The Communist mayor who is said
To be tough but fair
Is waiting.

Take me, silence.

GOING FAST

I

EXTRA HEARTBEATS

Red
As a Ducati 916, I'm crazed, I speed,
I blaze, I bleed,
I sight-read
A Bach Invention.

I'm at the redline.
When I speak you hear
The exhaust note of a privateer.

I see an audience of applause.
Pairs of hands in rows.
Palestinian and Jew.
And black and brown and yellow and red.
Wedding rings wearing watches
Pound lifelines into foam.
Fate lines. Date lines. Date palms. Politics. Foam.

The air blurs with the clapping.
The sidewalks sizzle with mica.
The colors tremble and vibrate.
The colors in the garden start to shake apart
While the applause swells.

The four walls of the world pump,
Pump their chemicals.

When I give my lectures,
The tachometer reads at the redline.
When I speak you hear
The exhaust note of a privateer.

The flutter in my chest is extra heartbeats,
My ectopy.

And Rabin is calling Arafat.
And Arafat, Rabin.
The touch-tone beeps are rising
To the sky like the bubbles in champagne.

The chemo is killing the white cells.
The white cells are killing the red cells.

They'll have to kill me first.

They'll find me
Flying on the floor.

II
CANDLE MADE FROM FAT

The most beautiful motorcycle ever made
Was just made.
I ride to Syria
To Assad on one.

A hundred and sixty-four miles an hour
On the 916
Makes a sound,
My friend, makes a sound.

I seek the most beautiful terror.
Massimo Tamburini designed it.
I ride to Syria
To President Assad on one.

Hafez al-Assad, a hundred and sixty-four miles an hour
On the Ducati 916
Makes a sound,
My friend, makes a certain sound.

A group that calls itself
The Other Woman,
In southern Lebanon, apparently with money
From Iran, is assembling the bomb.

It's red,
Flying through the desert
Toward the border with Israel,
As I approach my sixtieth birthday.

The school bus entering the outskirts
Of Jerusalem is full.
The motorcycle
Is screaming, God is great.

The kangaroo effect
Is boing-boing-boing as the white light bounds away,
Leaving in their blood the burning curls
Of Jewish boys and girls.

III

LAUDA, JERUSALEM

My violent Honda 125cc Grand Prix racer
Is the size of a bee.
It is too small to ride
Except for the joy.

My on-fire 1996 RS125R
Flies on its little wings,
A psalmist, all stinger,
On racing slicks.

It absolutely can't stop
Lifting its voice to scream.
It mounts the victory podium.
Lauda, Jerusalem, Dominum.

I am a Jew.
I am Japan.
I shift gears over and over.
I scream to victory again and again.

Fall leaves inflame the woods.
It is brilliant to live.
The sorrow that is not sorrow,
The mist of everything is over everything.

IV

POEM DOES

The god in the nitroglycerin
Is speedily absorbed under the tongue
Till it turns a green man red,
Which is what a poem does.
It explosively reanimates
By oxygenating the tribe.

No civilized state will execute
Someone who is ill
Till it makes the someone well
Enough to kill
In a civilized state,
As a poem does.

I run-and-bump the tiny
Honda 125cc Grand Prix racer. Only
Two steps and it screams. I
Slip the clutch to get the revs up, blipping and getting
Ready not to get deady,
Which also is what a poem does.

They dress them up in the retirement centers.
They dress them up in racing leathers.
They dress them up in war paint and feathers.
The autumn trees are in their gory glory.
The logs in the roaring fire keep passing
The peace pipe in pain, just what a poem does.

Stanza no. 5. We want to be alive.
Line 26. We pray for peace.
Line 27. The warrior and peacemaker Rabin is in heaven.
28. We don't accept his fate.
But we do. Life is going ahead as fast as it can,
Which is what a poem does.

V

ISRAEL

An animal in the wild
Comes up to you in a clearing because it
Has rabies. It loves you. It does not know why.
It pulls out a gun.
You really will die.

The motorcycle you are riding
Is not in control of itself.
It is not up to you to.
The sky is not well.
It wants to make friends.

It stalks you to
Hold out its hand
At a hundred and sixty-four miles an hour.
It asks you to
Take down your pants.

Daphne fleeing Apollo
Into the Sinai shrinks to a bonsai.
The Jewish stars that top the crown
Prime Minister Rabin is wearing
As he ascends to heaven assassinated, twinkle.

The main tank holds the dolphins.
Land for peace is not for them.
Daphne fleeing Apollo
Across the desert of your desk becomes
In India a cow.

The icing on the cake
Is stone. The Ten Commandments
Are incised in it.
You take a bite
Of Israel and spit out teeth, señor.

You throw your head back and wheelie
On the RS125R
And the Ducati,
Surrounded by security rushing you forward,
Suddenly aware you have been shot.

VI

KILLING HITLER

A Ducati Supermono walks down the aisle
At a hundred and forty-one miles an hour
To kiss the Torah, trumpeting,
An elephant downsized to a gazelle that devours lions.

Red Italian bodywork
Designed by the South African
Pierre Terblanche is sensuous lavish smoothness
With mustard-yellow highlights.

Even the instrument binnacle
Is beautiful and the green
Of the top triple clamp
Means magnesium, no expense spared, very trick.

The rabbi weighs only
301 lbs. with the tank full.
It wails straight
To the Wailing Wall.

It is big but being small
The Supermono has a mania.
The double con-rod balance system is elegance.
The total motorcycle bugles petite magnificence.

How to keep killing Hitler
Is the point.
How to be a work of art and win.
How to be Supermono and marry Lois Lane in the synagogue, and love.

From

The Cosmos Poems

(2000)

INTO THE EMPTINESS

Into the emptiness that weighs
More than the universe
Another universe begins
Smaller than the last.

Begins to smaller
Than the last.
Dimensions
Do not yet exist.

My friend, the darkness
Into which the seed
Of all eleven dimensions
Is planted is small.

Travel with me back
Before it grows to more.
The church bell bongs,
Which means it must be noon.

Some are playing hopscotch
Or skipping rope during recess,
And some are swinging on swings,
And seesaws are seesawing.

That she is shy,
Which means it must be May,
Turns into virgin snow
And walking mittened home with laughing friends.

And the small birds singing,
And the sudden silence,
And the curtains billow,
And the spring thunder will follow—

And the rush of freshness,
And the epileptic fit that foams.
The universe does not exist
Before it does.

INVISIBLE DARK MATTER

It is the invisible
Dark matter we are not made of
That I am afraid of.
Most of the universe consists of this.

I put a single normal ice cube
In my drink.
It weighs one hundred million tons.
It is a sample from the densest star.

I read my way across
The awe I wrote
That you are reading now.
I can't believe that you are there

Except you are. I wonder what
Cosmologists don't know
That could be everything
There is.

The someone looking at the page
Could be the everything there is,
Material that shines,
Or shined.

Dark matter is another
Matter. Cosmologists don't know.
The physicists do not.
The stars are not.

Another thing beside
The row of things is
Standing there. It is invisible,
And reads without a sound.

It doesn't matter
That it doesn't really.
I need to take its hand
To cross the street.

From

Life on Earth

(2001)

FREDERICK SEIDEL

I live a life of laziness and luxury,
Like a hare without a bone who sleeps in a pâté.
I met a fellow who was so depressed
He never got dressed and never got undressed.

He lived a life of laziness and luxury.
He hid his life away in poetry,
Like a hare still running from a gun in a pâté.
He didn't talk much about himself because there wasn't much to say.

He found it was impossible to look or not to.
It will literally blind him but he's got to.
Her caterpillar with a groove
Waits for love

Between her legs. The crease
Is dripping grease.
He's blind—now he really is.
Can't you help him, gods!

Her light is white
Moonlight.
Or the Parthenon under the sun
Is the other one.

There are other examples but
A perfect example in his poetry is the what
Will save you factor.
The Jaws of Life cut the life crushed in the compactor

Out.
My life is a snout
Snuffling toward the truffle, life. Anyway!
It is a life of luxury. Don't put me out of my misery.

I am seeking more Jerusalem, not less.
And in the outtakes, after they pull my fingernails out, I confess:
I do love
The sky above.

From

Ooga-Booga

(2006)

KILL POEM

Huntsman indeed is gone from Savile Row,
And Mr. Hall, the head cutter.
The red hunt coat Hall cut for me was utter
Red melton cloth thick as a carpet, cut just so.
One time I wore it riding my red Ducati racer—what a show!—
Matched exotics like a pair of lovely red egrets.
London once seemed the epitome of no regrets
And the old excellence one used to know
Of the chased-down fox bleeding its stink across the snow.

We follow blindly, clad in coats of pink,
A beast whose nature is to run and stink.
I am civilized in my pink but
Civilized is about having stuff.
The red coats are called "pinks." Too much is almost enough.
No one knows why they are. I parade in the air
With my stuff and watch the disappearing scut
Of a deer. I am civilized but
Civilized life is actually about too much.

I parade in the air
And wait for the New Year
That then will, then will disappear.
I am trying not to care.
I am not able not to.
A short erect tail
Winks across the winter field.
All will be revealed.
I am in a winter field.

They really are everywhere.
They crawl around in one's intimate hair.
They spread disease and despair.
They rape and pillage
In the middle of Sag Harbor Village.
They ferry Lyme disease.
The hunters' guns bring them to their knees.
In Paris I used to call the Sri Lankan servants "Shrees."
I am not able not to.

Winter, spring, Baghdad, fall,
Venery is written all
Over me like a rash,
Hair and the gash,
But also the Lehrer *NewsHour* and a wood fire and Bach.
A short erect tail
Winks across the killing field.
All will be revealed.
I am in a killing field.

I remember the *chasse à courre* in the forest in the Cher.
I remember the English thoroughbreds ridden by the frogs.
I remember the weeping stag cornered by the dogs.
The stag at bay in the pond literally shed a tear.
A hunt servant in a tricorn hat waded out to cut its throat.
Nelson Aldrich on his horse vomited watching this.
The huntsman's heraldic horn sounded the *hallali.*
The tune that cuts off the head. *L'hallali!*
Back to the château to drink the blood. *L'hallali!*

I am in Paris being introduced at Billy's,
1960, avenue Paul-Valéry.
One of her beautiful imported English Lillys or Millys
Is walking around on her knees.
It is rather like that line of Paul Valéry's.
Now get down on all fours, please.
We are ministers of state and then there is me chez Billy.
Deer garter-belt across our field of vision
And stand there waiting for our decision.

Our only decision was how to cook the venison.
I am civilized but
I see the silence
And write the words for the thought balloon.
When the woods are the color of a macaroon,
Deer, death is near.
I write about its looks in my books.
I write disappearing scut.
I write rut.

The title is *Kill Poetry*,
And in the book poetry kills.
In the poem the stag at bay weeps, literally.
Kill poetry is the *hallali* on avenue Paul-Valéry.
Get rid of poetry. Kill poetry.
Label on a vial of pills. Warning: Kill kill kill kills.
Its title is *Kill Poem*,
From the *Book of Kills*.
The antlered heads are mounted weeping all around the walls.

John F. Kennedy is mounted weeping on the wall.

His weeping brother Robert weeps nearby.

Martin Luther King, at bay in Memphis, exhausted, starts to cry.

His antlered head is mounted weeping on the wall.

Too much is almost enough, for crying out loud!

Bobby Kennedy announces to a nighttime crowd

That King has died, and then quotes Aeschylus, and then is killed.

Kill kill kill kills, appalls,

The American trophies covered in tears that deck the American halls.

VIOLIN

I often go to bed with a book
And immediately turn out the light.
I wake in the morning and brush and dress and go to the desk and write.
I always put my arm in the right sleeve before I slip into the left.
I always put on my left shoe first and then I put on the right.

I happen right now
To be walking the dogs in the dangerous park at night,
Which is dangerous, which I do not like,
But I am delighted, my dog walk is a delight.
I am right-handed but mostly I am not thinking.

(CHORUS)
A man can go to sleep one night and never wake up that he knows of.
A man can walk down a Baghdad street and never walk another drop.
A man can be at his publisher's and drop dead on the way to the men's room.
A poet can develop frontotemporal dementia.
A flavorful man can, and then he is not.

The call girls who came to our separate rooms were actually lovely.
Weren't they shocked that their customers were so illegally young?
Mine gently asked me what I wanted to do. Sin is Behovely.
Just then the phone rang—
Her friend checking if she was safe with the young Rambo, Rimbaud.

I am pursuing you, life, to the ends of the earth across a Sahara of tablecloth.
I look around the restaurant for breath.
I stuff my ears to sail past the siren song of the rocks.
The violin of your eyes
Is listening gently.

HOMAGE TO PESSOA

I once loved,
I thought I would be loved,
But I wasn't loved.
I wasn't loved for the only reason that matters—
It was not to be.
I unbuttoned my white gloves and stripped each off.
I set aside my gold-knobbed cane.
I picked up this pen . . .
And thought how many other men
Had smelled the rose in the bud vase
And lifted a fountain pen,
And lifted a mountain . . .
And put the shotgun in their mouth,
And noticed that their hunting dog was pointing.

FOG

I spend most of my time not dying.
That's what living is for.
I climb on a motorcycle.
I climb on a cloud and rain.
I climb on a woman I love.
I repeat my themes.

Here I am in Bologna again.
Here I go again.
Here I go again, getting happier and happier.
I climb on a log
Torpedoing toward the falls.
Basically, it sticks out of me.

At the factory,
The racer being made for me
Is not ready, but is getting deadly.
I am here to see it being born.
It is snowing in Milan, the TV says.
They close one airport, then both.

The Lord is my shepherd and the Director of Superbike Racing.
He buzzes me through three layers of security
To the innermost secret sanctum of the racing department
Where I will breathe my last.
Trains are delayed.
The Florence sky is falling snow.

Tonight Bologna is fog.
This afternoon, there it was,
With all the mechanics who are making it around it.
It stood on a sort of altar.
I stood in a sort of fog,
Taking digital photographs of my death.

A RED FLOWER

The poet stands on blue-veined legs, waiting for his birthday to be over.
He dangles from a muse who works the wires
That make a puppet move in lifelike ways onstage.
Happy birthday to a *semper paratus* penis!
His tiny Cartier wristwatch trumpets it!
He dares to wear a tiny thing that French and feminine.
Nose tilted up, arrogance, blue eyes.
He can smell the ocean this far inland.

We are in France. We are in Italy. We are in England. We are in heaven.
Lightning with a noose around its neck, feet on a cloud,
Drops into space, feet kicking, neck broken.
The parachute pops open . . . a red flower:
Plus ne suis ce que j'ai été,
Et plus ne saurais jamais l'être.
Mon beau printemps et mon été
Ont fait le saut par la fenêtre.

THE OWL YOU HEARD

The owl you heard hooting
In the middle of the night wasn't me.
It was an owl.
Or maybe you were
So asleep you didn't even hear it.
The sprinklers on their timer, programmed to come on
At such a strangely late hour in life
For watering a garden,
Refreshed your sleep four thousand miles away by
Hissing sweetly,
Deepening the smell of green in Eden.
You heard the summer chirr of insects.
You heard a sky of stars.
You didn't know it, fast asleep at dawn in Paris.
You didn't hear a thing.
You heard me calling.
I am no longer human.

E-MAIL FROM AN OWL

The irrigation system wants it to be known it *irrigates*
The garden,
It doesn't water it.
It is a stickler about this!
Watering is something done by hand.
Automated catering naturally
Does a better job than a hand with a watering can can.
Devised in Israel to irrigate their orange groves,
It gives life everywhere in the desert of life it goes.
It drips water to the chosen, one zone at a time.
Drip us this day our daily bread, or, rather, this night,
Since a drop on a leaf in direct sunlight can make
A magnifying glass that burns an innocent at the stake.
The sprinkler system hisses kisses on a timer
Under an exophthalmic sky of stars.
Tonight my voice will stare at you forever.
I click on Send,
And send you this perfumed magic hour.

DANTE'S BEATRICE

I ride a racer to erase her.
Bent over like a hunchback.
Racing leathers now include a hump
That protects the poet's spine and neck.
I wring the thing out, two hundred miles an hour.
I am a mink on a mink ranch determined not
To die inside its valuable fur, inside my racesuit.

I bought the racer
To replace her.
It became my slave and I its.
All it lacked was tits.
All it lacked
Between its wheels was hair.
I don't care.
We do it anyway.

The starter-caddy spins its raving little wheel
Against the Superbike's elevated fat black
Rear soft-compound tire.
Remember: *racer*—
Down for second gear instead of up!
Release the clutch—the engine fires.
I am off for my warm-up lap on a factory racer
Because I can't face her.

I ride my racer to erase her.
I ride in armor to
Three hundred nineteen kilometers an hour.
I am a mink on a mink ranch about
To die inside its valuable fur,
Inside my leathers.
She scoops me out to make a coat for her.
She buttons up a me of soft warm blur.

Is this the face that launched
A thousand slave ships?
The world is just outstanding.
My slavery never wavers.
I use the word "slavers"
To mean both "drools"
And, changing the pronunciation, "trades in slaves."
I consider myself most of these.

Mark Peploe and I used to sit around
Cafés in Florence grading
Muses' noses.
Hers hooks like Gauguin's,
His silent huge hooked hawk prow.
I am the cactus. You are the hyena.
I am the crash, you the fireball of Jet-A . . .
Only to turn catastrophe into dawn.

BOLOGNA

My own poetry I find incomprehensible.
Actually, I have no one.
Everything in art is couplets.
Mine don't rhyme.

Everything in the heart, you meant to say.
As if I ever meant to say anything.
Don't get me wrong.
I do without.

I find the poetry I write incomprehensible,
But at least I understand it.
It opens the marble
And the uniforms of the lobby staff

Behind the doorman at 834 Fifth.
Each elevator opens
On one apartment to a floor.
The elevator opened

To the page.
The elevator opened on the little vestibule
On the verge of something.
I hope I have. I hope I don't.

The vagina-eyed Modigliani nude
Made me lewd.
I waited for my friend to descend
The inner staircase of the duplex.

Keyword: house key.
You need a danger to be safe in.
Except in the African bush where you don't,
You do.

The doorway to my childhood
Was the daytime doorman.
An enormously black giant wore an outfit
With silver piping.

He wore a visored cap
With a high Gestapo peak
On his impenetrably black marble.
Waits out there in the sun to open the car door.

My noble Negro statue's name was Heinz,
My calmly grand George Washington.
You'll find me
At my beloved Hotel Baglioni

In Bologna
Still using the word Negro.
I need a danger to be safe in,
In room 221.

George Washington was calmly kind.
The defender of my building was George Washington
With a Nazi name
In World War II St. Louis.

Heinz stood in the terrible sun after
The Middle Passage in his nearly Nazi uniform.
He was my Master Race White Knight.
I was his white minnow.

The sun roars gloriously hot today.
Piazza Santo Stefano might as well be Brazzaville.
The humidity is a divinity.
Huck is happy on the raft in the divinity!

They show movies at night on an outdoor screen
In the steam in Piazza Maggiore.
I'm about to take a taxi
To Ducati

And see Claudio Domenicali, and see Paolo Ciabatti,
To discuss the motorcycle being made for me.
One of the eight factory Superbike racers
Ducati Corse will make for the year,

Completely by hand, will be mine.
I want to run racing slicks
On the street for the look,
Their powerful fat smooth black shine.

I need them
To go nowhere fast and get there.
I need to begin to
Write the poem of Colored Only.

When Heinz took my little hand in his,
Into the little vestibule on the verge
Of learning to ride a bicycle,
I began *Bologna*.

Federico Minoli of Bologna presides
In an unair-conditioned apartment fabulously
Looking out on the seven churches
In Piazza Santo Stefano, in the town center.

The little piazza opens
A little vestibule on the verge of something.
The incredible staircase to his place opens
On seven churches at the top.

The only problem is the bongo drums at night.
Ducati's president and CEO is the intelligent Federico.
Late tonight I will run into him and his wife
At Cesarina, in the brown medieval

Piazza, a restaurant Morandi
Used to lunch at,
Bologna's saintly pure painter of stillness.
I will sit outside in the noisy heat and eat.

CLOCLO

The golden person curled up on my doormat,
Using her mink coat as a blanket,
Blondly asleep, a smile on her face, was my houseguest
The Goat who couldn't get her set of keys to work, so blithely
Bedded down to wait in the apartment outside hall.
A natural animal elegance physically
Released a winged ethereal exuberance,
Pulling g's, then weightlessness, the charm of the divine,
Luxuriously asleep in front of the front door like a dog.
Dear polymorphous goddess who past sixty
Could still instantly climb a tree,
But couldn't get the metal key
To turn in any residence
In London or New York or Calabria or Greece or Florence.
Always climbing anything (why
Someone had dubbed her the Goat when she was young),
Climbing everywhere in a conversation,
Up the Nile, up the World Trade Center Twin Towers,
Upbeat, up late, up at dawn, up for anything,
Up the ladder to the bells.
A goat saint lived ravishingly on a rock,
Surrounded by light, dressed in a simple frock,
The last great puritan aesthete
In the Cyclades.
She painted away
Above the Greek blue sea.
She chatted away
Beneath the Greek blue sky.
Every year returned to London.
So European. So Jamesian.

Every year went back

To Florence, her first home.

To the thirty-foot-high stone room in Bellosguardo.

To paint in the pearl light the stone gave off.

Ten generations after Leonardo had painted on the same property.

She worked hard as a nun

On her nude landscapes of the south,

With their occasional patio or dovecote and even green bits,

But never people or doves, basking in the sun.

Believed only in art.

Believed in tête-à-têtes.

Believed in walks to the top of the hill.

Knew all the simple people, and was loved.

It comes through the telephone

From Florence when I call that she has died quietly a minute ago,

Like a tear falling in a field of snow,

Climbing up the ladder to the bells out of Alzheimer's total whiteout,

Heavenly Clotilde Peploe called by us all Cloclo.

BARBADOS

Literally the most expensive hotel in the world
Is the smell of rain about to fall.
It does the opposite, a grove of lemon trees.
I isn't anything.
It is the hooks of rain
Hovering with their sweets inches off the ground.
I is the spiders marching through the air.
The lines dangle the bait
The ground will bite.
Your wife is as white as vinegar, pure aristo privilege.
The excellent smell of rain before it falls overpowers
The last aristocrats on earth before the asteroid.
I sense your disdain, darling.
I share it.

The most expensive hotel in the world
Is the slave ship unloading Africans on the moon.
They wear the opposite of space suits floating off the dock
To a sugar mill on a hilltop.
They float into the machinery.
The machine inside the windmill isn't vegetarian.
A "lopper" lops off a limb caught
In the rollers and the machine never has to stop.
A black arm turns into brown sugar,
And the screaming rest of the slave keeps the other.
His African screams can't be heard above the roar.
A spaceship near the end of a voyage was becalmed.
Two astronauts floated weightlessly off the deck
Overboard into the equator in their chains and *splash* and drowned.

A cane toad came up to them.

They'd never seen anything so remarkable.

Now they could see the field was full of them.

Suddenly the field is filled with ancestors.

The hippopotamuses became friendly with the villagers.

Along came white hunters who shot the friendly hippos dead.

If they had known that friendship would end like that,

They never would have entered into it.

Suddenly the field is filled with souls.

The field of sugarcane is filled with hippopotamus cane toads.

They always complained

Our xylophones were too loud.

The Crocodile King is dead.

The world has no end.

The crocodile explodes out of the water and screams at the crowd

That one of them has stolen his mobile phone.

On the banks of the muddy Waddo, *ooga-booga!*

What about a Christmas tree in a steamy lobby on the Gulf of Guinea!

Because in Africa there are Africans

And they are Africans and are in charge.

Even obstipation

Can't stop a mighty nation.

The tragic magic makes lightning.

Some of the young captives are unspeakable

In their beauty, and their urine makes lightning, black and gold.

The heat is so hot

It will boil you in a pot.

Diarrhea in a condom is the outcome.

The former president completely loses it and screams from the stage
That someone fucking stole his fucking phone.
The audience of party faithful is terrified and giggles.
This was their man who brought the crime rate down
By executing everyone.
The crocodile staged a coup
And ended up in prison himself
And then became the president.
He stood for quality of life and clitorectomy.
But in his second term, in order to secure those international loans,
The crocodile changed his spots to free speech.
Lightning sentences them at birth to life without parole
With no time off for good behavior.
At that point in the voyage the ocean turns deeper.

People actually suffered severe optical damage from the blinding effects
Of the white roads in full sunlight.
It is the island roads so white you can't see,
Made of crushed limestone snow.
It is the tropical rain the color of grapefruit
Hovering in the figure of the goddess Niscah
Above the tile roof of the plantation house.
She dangles her baited lines.
It is the black of the orchids in a vase.
The goddess overpowers the uprising
And *I* is the first one hacked to pieces.
The asteroid is coming to the local cinema.
It is a moonlit night with the smell of rain in the air.
Thump thump, speed bump.

The most expensive hotel in the world ignites
As many orgasms as there are virgins in paradise.
These epileptic foaming fits dehydrate one,
But justify the cost of a honeymoon.
The Caribbean is room temperature,
Rippling over sand as rich as cream.
The beach chair has the thighs of a convertible with the top down.
You wave a paddle and the boy
Runs to take your order.
Many things are still done barefoot.
Others have the breakout colors of a parrot.
In paradise it never rains, but smells as if it could.
Two who could catapulted themselves overboard into the equator.
I die of thirst and drown in chains, in love.

Into the coconut grove they go. *Into the coconut grove they go.*
The car in the parking lot is theirs. *The car in the parking lot is theirs.*
The groves of lemon trees give light. *Ooga-booga!*
The hotel sheds light. *Ooga-booga!*
The long pink-shell sky of meaning wanted it to be, but really,
The precious thing is that they voted. *Ooga-booga!* And there we were,
The cane toads and the smell of rain about to fall.
The crocodiles and spiders are
The hippos and their friends who shot them dead.
The xylophone is playing too loud
Under the coconut palms, which go to the end of the world.
The slave is screaming too loud and we
Can't help hearing
Our tribal chant and getting up to dance under the mushroom cloud.

CLIMBING EVEREST

The young keep getting younger, but the old keep getting younger.
But this young woman is young. We kiss.
It's almost incest when it gets to this.
This is the consensual, national, metrosexual hunger-for-younger.

I'm getting young.
I'm totally into strapping on the belt of dynamite
Which will turn me into light.
God is great! I suck Her tongue.

I mean—my sunbursts, and there are cloudbursts.
My dynamite penis
Is totally into Venus.
My penis in Venus hungers and thirsts,

It burns and drowns.
My dynamite penis
Is into Venus.
The Atlantic off Sagaponack is freezing black today and frowns.

I enter the jellyfish folds
Of floating fire.
The mania in her labia can inspire
Extraordinary phenomena and really does cure colds.

It holds the Tower of Pisa above the freezing black waves.
The mania is why
I mention I am easily old enough to die,
And actually it's the mania that saves

The Tower from falling over.
Climbing Everest is the miracle—which leaves the descent
And reporting to the world from an oxygen tent
In a soft pasture of cows and clover.

Happening girls parade around my hospice bed.
The tented canopy means I am in the rue de Seine in Paris.
It will embarrass
Me in Paris to be dead.

It's Polonius embarrassed behind the arras,
And the arras turning red.
Hamlet has outed Polonius and Sir Edmund Hillary will wed
Ophelia in Paris.

Give me Everest or give me death.
Give me altitude with an attitude.
But I am naked and nude.
I am constantly out of breath.

A naked woman my age is just a total nightmare,
But right now one is coming through the door
With a mop, to mop up the cow flops on the floor.
She kisses the train wreck in the tent and combs his white hair.

BROADWAY MELODY

A naked woman my age is a total nightmare.
A woman my age naked is a nightmare.
It doesn't matter. One doesn't care.
One doesn't say it out loud because it's rare
For anyone to be willing to say it,
Because it's the equivalent of buying billboard space to display it,

Display how horrible life after death is,
How horrible to draw your last breath is,
When you go on living.
I hate the old couples on their walkers giving
Off odors of love, and in City Diner eating a ray
Of hope, and then paying and trembling back out on Broadway,

Drumming and dancing, chanting something nearly unbearable,
Spreading their wings in order to be more beautiful and more terrible.

THE BLACK-EYED VIRGINS

A terrorist rides the rails underwater
From one language to another in a packed train of London
Rugby fans on their way to the big match in Paris
And a flock of Japanese schoolgirls ready to be fucked
In their school uniforms in paradise.
This is all just after Madrid in the reign of terror.
This is the girls' first trip outside Japan.
The terrorist swings in the hammock of their small skirts and black socks.
The chunnel train stops in the tunnel with an announcement
That everyone now alive is already human remains.
The terrorists have seen to it that trains
Swap human body parts around with bombs.
The Japanese schoolgirls say so sorry.
Their new pubic hair is made of light.

EUROSTAR

Japanese schoolgirls in their school uniforms with their school chaperones
Ride underwater on a train
Every terrorist in the world would dearly love to bomb
For the publicity and to drown everybody.
The Eurostar dashes into the waves.
The other passengers are watching the Japanese girls eat
Little sweeties they bought with their own money
In London. President Bush the younger is making ice cream.
Ice cream for dessert
Is what Iraq is, without the courses that normally come before.
You eat dessert to start and then you have dessert.
One of them is a Balthus in her short school skirt standing on the seat.
She reaches up too high to get something out of her bag.
She turns around smiling because she knows where you are looking.

DRINKING IN THE DAYTIME

Anything is better than this
Bliss.
Nursing on a long-stemmed bubble made of crystal.
I'm sucking on the barrel of a crystal pistol
To get a bullet to my brain.
I'm gobbling a breast, drinking myself down the drain.

I'm in such a state of Haut-Brion I can't resist.
A fist-fucking anus swallowing a fist.
You're wondering why I talk this way, so daintily!
I'll tell you after I take a pee.
Now I'm back.
Oilcoholics love the breast they attack.

I'm talking about the way poetry made me free.
It's treated me very well, you see.
I climbed up inside the Statue of Liberty
In the days when you could still go up in the torch, and that was me.
I mean every part I play.
I'm drinking my lunch at Montrachet.

I'm a case of Haut-Brion turning into tar.
I'm talking about the recent war.
It's a case of having to raise your hand in life to be
Recognized so you can ask your question. *Mr. Secretary! Mr. Secretary!*
To the secretary of defense, I say:
I lift my tar to you at Montrachet!

I lift my lamp beside the golden door to pee,

And make a vow to make men free, and we will find their WMD.

Sir, I supported the war.

I believe in who we are.

I dedicate red wine to that today.

At Montrachet, near the Franklin Street stop, on West Broadway.

THE DEATH OF THE SHAH

Here I am, not a practical man,
But clear-eyed in my contact lenses,
Following no doubt a slightly different line than the others,
Seeking sexual pleasure above all else,
Despairing of art and of life,
Seeking protection from death by seeking it
On a racebike, finding release and belief on two wheels,
Having read a book or two,
Having eaten well,
Having traveled not everywhere in sixty-seven years but far,
Up the Eiffel Tower and the Leaning Tower of Pisa
And the World Trade Center Twin Towers
Before they fell,
Mexico City, Kuala Lumpur, Accra,
Tokyo, Berlin, Teheran under the Shah,
Cairo, Bombay, L.A., London,
Into the jungles and the deserts and the cities on the rivers
Scouting locations for the movie,
A blue-eyed white man with brown hair,
Here I am, a worldly man,
Looking around the room.

Any foal in the kingdom
The Shah of Iran wanted
He had brought to him in a military helicopter
To the palace.
This one was the daughter of one of his ministers, all legs, a goddess.
She waited in a room.
It was in the afternoon.

I remember mounds of caviar before dinner
In a magnificent torchlit tent,
An old woman's beautiful house, a princess,
Three footmen for every guest,
And a man who pretended to get falling-down drunk
And began denouncing the Shah,
And everyone knew was a spy for the Shah.
A team of New York doctors (mine among them)
Was flown to Mexico City to consult.
They were not allowed to examine the Shah.
They could ask him how he felt.

The future of psychoanalysis
Is a psychology of surface.
Stay on the outside side.
My poor analyst
Suffered a stroke and became a needy child.
As to the inner life: let the maid.

How pathetic is a king who died of cancer
Rushing back after all these years to consult more doctors.
Escaped from the urn of his ashes in his pajamas.
Except in Islam you are buried in your body.
The Shah mounts the foal.
It is an honor.
He is in and out in a minute.
She later became my friend
And married a Texan.

I hurry to the gallery on the last day of the show
To a line stretching around the block in the rain—
For the Shah of sculptors, sculpture's virile king,
And his cold-rolled steel heartless tons.
The blunt magnificence stuns.
Cruelty has a huge following.
The cold-rolled steel mounts the foal.

The future of psychoanalysis is it has none.

I carry a swagger stick.
I eat a chocolate.
I eat brown blood.

When we drove with our driver on the highways of Ghana
To see for ourselves what the slave trade was,
Elmina was Auschwitz.
The slaves from the bush were marched to the coast
And warehoused in dungeons under St. George's Castle,
Then FedExed to their new jobs far away.
One hotel kept a racehorse as a pet.
The owner allowed it the run of the property.
Very shy, it walked standoffishly
Among the hotel guests on the walkways and under the palms.
The Shah had returned as a racehorse dropping mounds of caviar
Between a coconut grove and the Gulf of Guinea.

An English royal is taught to strut
With his hands clasped behind his back.
A racehorse in West Africa kept as a pet
Struts the same way the useless royals do,
Nodding occasionally to indicate he is listening.
His coat has been curried until he is glistening.

Would you rather be a horse without a halter
Than one winning races being whipped?
The finish line is at the starting gate, at St. George's Castle.
The starting gate is at the finish line for the eternal life.
God rears and whinnies and gives a little wave.
He would rather be an owner than a slave.

Someone fancy says
How marvelous money is.
Here I am, an admirer of Mahatma Gandhi,
Ready to praise making pots of money
And own a slave.
I am looking in the mirror as I shave the slave.
I shave the Shah.
I walk into the evening and start being charming.

A counterfeiter prints me.
(The counterfeiter *is* me.)
He prints Mohammad Reza Shah Pahlavi.

I call him Nancy.
He is so fancy.
It is alarming
He is so charming.
It is the thing he does and knows.
It is the fragrance of a rose.
It is the nostrils of his nose.
It is the poetry and prose.
It is the poetry.
It is a horse cab ride through Central Park when it snows.
It is Jackie Kennedy's hairpiece that came loose,
That a large Secret Service agent helped reattach.

I remember the Duck and Duckess of Windsor.
You could entertain them in your house.

Here I am, looking around the room
At everyone getting old except the young,
Discovering that I am lacking in vanity,
Not that I care, being debonair,
Delighted by an impairment of feeling
That keeps everything away,
People standing around in a display case
Even when they are in bed with you,
And laser-guided bombs destroy the buildings
Inside the TV, not that I care,
Not that I do not like it all,
Not that I am short or tall,
Not that I do not like to be alive,
And I appeal to you for pity,
Having in mind that you will read this
Under circumstances I cannot imagine
A thousand years from now.

Have pity on a girl, perdurable, playful,
And delicate as a foal, dutiful, available,
Who is waiting on a bed in a room in the afternoon for God.
His Majesty is on his way, who long ago has died.
She is a victim in the kingdom, and is proud.
Have pity on me a thousand years from now when we meet.
Open the mummy case of this text respectfully.
You find no one inside.

From

Evening Man

⊡

(2008)

BOYS

Sixty years after, I can see their smiles,
White with Negro teeth, and big with good,
When one or the other brought my father's Cadillac out
For us at the Gatesworth Garage.
RG and MC were the godhead,
The older brothers I dreamed I had.
I didn't notice they were colored,
Because older boys capable of being kind
To a younger boy are God.
It is absolutely odd
To be able to be with God.
I can almost see their faces, but can't quite.
I remember how blazingly graceful they were,
And that they offered to get me a girl so I could meet God.

I have an early memory of a black chauffeur,
Out of his livery,
Hosing down a long black Packard sedan, sobbing.
Did it happen? It took place
In Portland Place.
I remember the pink-soled gum boots
That went with the fellow's very pink gums
And very white teeth, while he washed
The Packard's whitewalls white
And let them dry, sobbing,
Painting on liquid white with an applicator afterward.
Later that afternoon he resumed his chauffeur costume,
A darky clad in black under the staring sun.
Franklin Delano Roosevelt had died.

On the other hand, Ronny Banks was light-skinned.
He worked as a carhop at Medart's drive-in.
He was well-spoken, gently friendly.
He was giving a party, but I didn't go.
I actually drove there, but something told me no.
I suddenly thought he was probably a homo.
I drank my face off, age fifteen.
I hit the bars
In the colored section to hear jazz.
I raved around the city in my father's cars,
A straight razor who, wherever he kissed, left scars.
I was violently heterosexual and bad.
I used every bit of energy I had.
Where, I wonder, is Ronny Banks now?

I remember a young man, whose name I have forgotten,
Who was exceedingly neat,
Always wearing a white shirt,
Always standing there jet-black in our living room.
How had this been allowed to happen?
Who doesn't hate a goody-goody young Christian?
My father and uncle underwrote the boy's education.
He was the orphaned son of a minister.
He sang in the church choir.
He was exemplary, an exemplar.
But justice was far away, very far.
Justice was really an ashtray to display
The lynched carcass of a stubbed-out cigar,
Part brown, part black, part stink, part ash.

When I was a little boy,
My father had beautiful manners,
A perfect haughty gentleman,
Impeccable with everyone.
In labor relations with the various unions,
For example, he apparently had no peer.
It was not so much that he was generous,
I gather, but rather that he was fair.
So it was a jolt, a jolt of joy,
To hear him cut the shit
And call a black man Boy.
The white-haired old Negro was a shoeshine boy.
One of the sovereign experiences of my life was my joy
Hearing my father in a fury call the man Boy.

Ronny Banks, faggot prince, where are you now?
RG and MC, are you already under headstones
That will finally reveal your full
Names, whatever they were?
RG, the younger brother, was my hero who was my friend.
I remember our playing
Catch in the rain for hours on a rainy weekend.
It is a question
Of when, not a question of whether,
The glory of the Lord shall be revealed
And all flesh shall cease together.
A black woman came up to my father.
All the colored people in this city know who you are.
God sent you to us. Thank God for your daddy, boy.

"SII ROMANTICO, SEIDEL, TANTO PER CAMBIARE"

Women have a playground slide
That wraps you in monsoon and takes you for a ride.
The English girl Louise, his latest squeeze, was being snide.
Easy to deride
The way he stayed alive to stay inside
His women with his puffed-up pride.
The pharmacy supplied
The rising fire truck ladder that the fire did not provide.
The toothless carnivore devoured Viagra and Finasteride
(Which is the one that shrinks the American prostate nationwide
And at a higher dosage grows hair on the bald) to stem the tide.
Not to die had been his way to hide
The fact that he was terrified.
He could not tell them that, it would be suicide.
It would make them even *more* humidified.
The women wrapped monsoon around him, thunder-thighed.
They guide his acetone to their formaldehyde.
Now Alpha will commit Omegacide.
He made them, like a doctor looking down a throat, open wide,
Say Ah; and *Ah*, they sighed;
And out came sighing amplified
To fill a stadium with cyanide.
He filled the women with rodenticide.
He tied
Their wrists behind them, tried
Ball gags in their mouths, and was not satisfied.
The whole room when the dancing started clapped and cried.
The bomber was the bomb, and many died.
The unshod got their feet back on and ran outside.
The wedding party bled around the dying groom and bride.

BIPOLAR NOVEMBER

I get a phone call from my dog who died,
But I don't really.
I don't hear anything.
Dear Jimmy, it is hard.
Dear dog, you were just a dog.
I am returning your call.

I have nothing to say.
I have nothing to add.
I have nothing to add to that.
I am saying hello to no.
How do you do, no!
I am returning your call.

I rode a bubble to the surface just now.
I unthawed the unthawed.
I said yes. Yes, yes,
How do you do?
I called to say hello
But am happy.

Today it is spring in November.
The weather opens the windows.
The windows look pretty dirty.
I go to my computer to see.
The six-day forecast calls
For happy haze for six days.

The trees look like they're budding.
They can't be in late November.
It is mucilaginous springtime.
It is all beginning all over.
The warplanes levitate
To take another crack at Iraq.

Hey, Mr. Big Shot!
I bet you went to Harvard.
Leaves are still on the trees.
The trees are wearing fine shoes.
Everything is handmade.
Everything believes.

ITALY

TO JONATHAN GALASSI

My last summer on earth
I spent admiring Milan,
But they were having a heat wave.
The Japanese were everywhere.
They eat lice.
They order *risotto milanese*.
They eat everything.
My cell phone has changed my life.
I never talk to anyone.

I spent the summer in Bologna.
Bologna is my town.
Bologna is so brown.
I ate shavings
Of tuna roe on buttered toast
Despite the heat,
Brown waxy slices of fishy salt
As strong as ammonia, Bologna.
Bologna, it takes a prince to eat *bottarga*.

Italy, your women are Italian!
Your motorcycles are women.
Milan, your men are high-heeled women.
Bologna, your brown arcades
Are waterfalls of shade.
Fascist Italy was ice cream in boots.
Its *crema* straddled the world.
It licked south in the heat.
It licked its boot.

Fascisti! They take American Express!
Comunisti! You forgot to sign!
I have my table at Rodrigo in Bologna.
I always eat at Bice in Milan.
It is sweet to eat at Bibe, outside Florence,
To walk there from Bellosguardo through the fields.
Montale's little Bibe poem is printed on the menu.
I write my own.
Islam is coming.

MU'ALLAQA

FOR IMRU' AL-QAYS

The elephant's trunk uncurling
From the lightning flashes
In the clouds was Marie Antoinette,
As usual trumpeting.
The greedy suction
Was her tornado vacuuming across the golden Kansas flatness.

Meanwhile, the count was talking to the swan.
The swan liked what he was saying and got
Right out of the pond.
Meanwhile, grown men in Afghanistan.
The count had fought in Algeria.
Meanwhile, neon in Tokyo.

Madame la Comtesse waved to us from the top step,
Waved to her count, their swan, their ornamental pond, *et moi*.
We were a towering cornucopia
Of autumn happiness
And *gourmandise* rotating counterclockwise,
Backwards toward the guillotine.

I kept a rainbow as a pet and grandly
Walked the rainbow on a leash.
I exercised it evenings together with the cheetah,
A Thorstein Veblen moment of conspicuous consumption:
A dapper dauphin in a T-shirt that said FRED
Parading with his pets decked out in T-shirts that said FRED'S.

I left my liver in the Cher.
I ate my heart out *en Berry*.
We drank and ate
France between the wars,
And every morning couldn't wait.
It felt sunshiny in the shadow of the château.

And when the rainbow leapt from there to here,
It landed twenty years away from the Cher.
The place it landed was the Persian Gulf.
It landed twinkling stardust where I'm standing in my life
With one-hump Marie Antoinette, my wife,
Who resembles that disarming camel yesterday.

In fact, the camel yesterday was smitten.
She left the other camels to come over.
You have a lovely liquid wraparound eye.
She stood there looking at me sideways.
They feed their racing camels caviar in Qatar.
The ruler of Dubai has said that he will try to buy Versailles.

A refrigerated ski slope, five stories high,
Lives improbably inside a downtown shopping mall in Dubai.
Arab men, wearing sneakers under their robes, hold hands.
Faceless black veils stop shopping to watch through the glass.
Seeing the skiers emphasizes the desert,
Like hearing far-off thunder at a picnic.

Both the word *thunder* and the word *picnic* are of course Arabic.
Indeed, Arabic was the language of French aristocrats
Before the Terror, bad body odor perfumed.
It is the language of the great Robert Frost poems,
Which have the suicide bomber's innocence
Walking safely past the checkpoint into the crowd.

They pay payola to Al Qaeda to stay away from Doha.
The emir was in his counting-house, counting out his oil and gas.
Another sunny Sunni day in the UAE!
A candidate for president
Who wants to manumit our oil-dependent nation
First has to get the message to every oily girl and boy

To just say no to up and down and in and out, labanotation
Of moaning oil rigs extracting oil joy.
My fellow Americans, I see a desert filled with derricks
Pumping up and down but never satisfied:
Obsessional hydraulics and Jimi Hendrix has hysterics.
I smash my guitar to bits onstage and that's all, folks!

It isn't.
I contemplate the end of the world. It isn't.
I have my croissant and café and the *Trib* and walk the rainbow
Around the block.
The young North African hipsters in the bitter *banlieues*
Contemplate the end of the world.

I contemplate the end of the world but in my case
It's not.
There are still things to buy.
I walk the rainbow in the dark.
The world is the kiosk where I get my *Herald Tribune*.
The world is my local café where my café au lait is quadroon.

I go to the strange little statue of Pierre Mendès-France
In the jardin du Luxembourg, in Paris, France.
I make a pilgrimage to it.
My quaint political saint and I visit.
The young North African hipsters in the bitter *banlieues*
Contemplate the end of the world, which isn't

The end of the world, though yes, quite true,
In Algeria and Afghanistan
Jihad is developing a dirty nuclear bomb
That smells like frangipani in flower
To keep Frangipani in power.
Ayatollah Frangipani has returned from his long exile in France

To annihilate vice.
I stomp the campfire out and saddle up my loyal *Mayflower*—
Who is swifter than a life is brief under the stars!
My prize four-wheel-drive with liquid wraparound eyes!
We ski the roller-coaster ocean's up and down dunes.
We reach land at last and step on Plymouth Rock.

EVENING MAN

The man in bed with me this morning is myself, is me,
The sort of same-sex marriage New York State allows.
Both men believe in infidelity.
Both wish they could annul their marriage vows.

This afternoon I will become the Evening Man,
Who does the things most people only dream about.
He swims around his women like a swan, and spreads his fan.
You can't drink that much port and not have gout.

In point of fact, it is arthritis.
His drinking elbow aches, and he admits to this.
To be a candidate for higher office,
You have to practice drastic openness.

You have to practice looking like thin air
When you become the way you do not want to be,
An ancient head of ungrayed dark brown hair
That looks like dyed fur on a wrinkled monkey.

Of course, the real vacation we will take is where we're always headed.
Presidents have Air Force One to fly them there.
I run for office just to get my dark brown hair beheaded.
I wake up on a slab, beheaded, in a White House somewhere.

Evening Man sits signing bills in the Oval Office headless—
Every poem I write starts or ends like this.
His hands have been chopped off. He signs bills with the mess.
The country is in good hands. It ends like this.

POEM BY THE BRIDGE AT TEN-SHIN

This jungle poem is going to be my last.
This space walk is.
Racing in a cab through springtime Central Park,
I kept my nose outside the window like a dog.
The stars above my bed at night are vast.
I think it is uncool to call young women Ms.
My darling is a platform I see stars from in the dark,
And all the dogs begin to bark.
My grunting gun brings down her charging warthog,
And she is frying on white water, clinging to a log,
And all the foam and fevers shiver.
And drink has made chopped liver of my liver!
Between my legs it's Baudelaire.
He wrote about her Central Park of hair.

I look for the *minuterie* as if I were in France,
In darkness, in the downstairs entrance, looking for the light.
I'm on a timer that will give me time
To see the way and up the stairs before the lights go out.
The so delicious Busby Berkeley dancers dance
A movie musical extravaganza on the staircase with me every night.
Such fun! We dance. We climb. We slip in slime.
We're squirting squeezes like a wedge of lime!
It's like a shout.
It's what *minuterie* is all about.
Just getting to the landing through the dark
That has been interrupted for a minute is a lark.
And she's so happy. It is grand!
I put my mobile in her ampersand.

The fireworks are a fleeting puff of sadness.
The flowers when they reach the stars are tears.
I don't remember poems I write.
I turn around and they are gone.
I do remember poor King Richard Nixon's madness.
Pierre Leval, we loved those years!
We knocked back shots of single malt all night.
Beer chasers gave *dos caballeros* double vision, second sight—
Twin putti pissing out the hotel window on the Scottish dawn.
A crocodile has fallen for a fawn.
I live flap copy for a children's book.
He wants to lick. He wants to look.
A tiny goldfinch is his Cupid.
Love of cuntry makes men stupid.

It makes men miss Saddam Hussein!
Democracy in Baghdad makes men think
Monstrosity was not so bad.
I followed Gandhi barefoot to
Remind me there is something else till it began to rain.
The hurricane undressing of democracy in Baghdad starts to sink
The shrunken page size of *The New York Times*, and yet we had
A newspaper that mattered once, and that is sad,
But that was when it mattered. Do
I matter? That is true.
I don't matter but I do. I lust for fame,
And after never finding it I never was the same.
I roared into the heavens and I soared,
And landed where I started on a flexing diving board.

I knew a beauty named Dawn Green.
I used to wake at the crack of Dawn.
I wish I were about to land on Plymouth Rock,
And had a chance to do it all again but do it right.
It was green dawn in pre-America. I mean
Great scented forests all along the shore, which now are gone.
I've had advantages in life and I pronounce Iraq "Irrock."
The right schools taught me how to tock.
I'm tocking Turkey to the Kurds but with no end in sight.
These peace tocks are my last. Goodbye, Iran. Iran, good night.
They burned the undergrowth so they could see the game they hunt.
That made the forest a cathedral clear as crystal like a cunt.
Their arrows entered red meat in the glory
Streaming down from the clerestory.

Carine Rueff, I was obsessed—I was *possessed!* I liked your name.
I liked the fact Marie Christine Carine Rue F was Jewish.
It emphasized your elegance in Paris and in Florence.
You were so blond in rue de l'Université!
The dazzling daughter of de Gaulle's adviser Jacques Rueff was game
For anything. I'm lolling here in Mayfair under bluish
Clouds above a bench in Mount Street Gardens, thinking torrents.
Purdey used to make a gun for shooting elephants.
One cannot be the way one was back then today.
It went away.
I go from Claridge's to Brands Hatch racing circuit and come back
To Claridge's, and out and eat and drink and bed, and fade to black.
The elephants were old enough to die but were aghast.
The stars above this jungle poem are vast.

To Ninety-second Street and Broadway I have come.
Outside the windows is New York.
I came here from St. Louis in a covered wagon overland
Behind the matchless prancing pair of Eliot and Ezra Pound.
And countless moist oases took me in along the way, and some
I still remember when I lift my knife and fork.
The Earth keeps turning, night and day, spit-roasting all the tanned
Tired icebergs and the polar bears, which makes white almost contraband.
The biosphere on a rotisserie emits a certain sound
That tells the stars that Earth was moaning pleasure while it drowned.
The amorous white icebergs flash their brown teeth, hissing.
They're watching old porn videos of melting icebergs pissing.
The icebergs still in panty hose are lesbians and kissing.
The rotting ocean swallows the bombed airliner that's missing.

From

Nice Weather

◻

(2012)

NIGHT

The city sleeps with the lights on.
The insomniac wants it to be morning.
The quadruple amputee asks the night nurse what time it is.
The woman is asking for her mother,
But the mother is exhausted and asleep and long since dead.
The nun screams to stop the charging rhino
And sits bolt upright in bed
Attached to a catheter.

If a mole were afraid of the dark
Underground, its home, afraid of the dark,
And climbed out into the light of day, utterly blind,
Destroying the lawn, it would probably be caught and shot,
But not in the recovery room after a craniotomy.
The prostitute suspects what her client might want her to do.
Something is going on. Something is wrong.
Meanwhile, the customer is frightened, too.

The city sleeps with the lights on.
The garbage trucks come in the night and make noise and are gone.
Two angelfish swim around the room and out the window.
Laundry suns on a line beneath white summer cumulus.
Summer thunder bumbles in the distance.
The prostitute—whose name is Dawn—
Takes the man in her mouth and spits out blood,
Rosy-fingered Dawn.

STORE WINDOWS

I smile in the mirror at my teeth—
Which are their usual brown.
My smile is wearing a wreath.
I walk wreathed in brown around town.
I smile and rarely frown.

I find perfection in
The passing store windows
I glance at my reflection in.
It's citywide narcissism. Citizens steal a little peek, and what it shows
Is that every ugly lightbulb in that one moment glows.

A preposterous example: I'm getting an ultrasound
Of my carotid artery,
And the woman doing it, a tough transplanted Israeli, bends around
And says huskily, "Don't tell anybody
I said that your carotid is extraordinary."

I'm so proud!
It's so ridiculous I have to laugh.
The technician is very well endowed.
I'm a collapsible top hat—a *chapeau claque*—that half
The time struts around at Ascot but can be collapsed flat just like that. *Baff!*

Till it pops back. *Paff!* Oh yes,
I find myself superb
When I undress.
A lovely lightbulb is my suburb,
And my flower, and my verb.

The naked man, after climbing the steps out of the subway,
Has moderate dyspnea, and is seventy-four.
He was walking down the street in Milan one day.
This was long ago. He began to snore.
He saw a sleeping man reflected in the window of a store.

DOWNTOWN

July 4th fireworks exhale over the Hudson sadly.
It is beautiful that they have to disappear.
It's like the time you said I love you madly.
That was an hour ago. It's been a fervent year.
I don't really love fireworks, not really, the flavorful floating shroud
In the nighttime sky above the river and the crowd.
This time, because of the distance upriver perhaps, they're not loud,
Even the colors aren't, the patterns getting pregnant and popping.
They get bigger and louder when they start stopping.
They try to rally
At the finale.
It's the four-hundredth anniversary of Henry Hudson's discovery—
Which is why the fireworks happen on this side of the island this year.
Shad are back, and we celebrate the Hudson's Clean Water Act recovery.
What a joy to eat the unborn. We're monsters, I fear. What monsters we're.
We'll binge on shad roe next spring in the delicious few minutes it's here.

BEFORE AIR-CONDITIONING

The sweetness of the freshness of the breeze!
The wind is wiggling the trees.
The sky is black. The trees deep green.
The man mowing the enormous lawn before it rains makes goodness clean.
It's the smell of laundry on the line
And the smell of the sea, brisk iodine,
Nine hundred miles inland from the ocean, it's that smell.
It makes someone little who has a fever feel almost well.
It's exactly what a sick person needs to eat.
Maybe it's coming from Illinois in the heat.
Watch out for the crows, though.
With them around, caw, caw, it's going to snow.
I think I'm still asleep. I hope I said my prayers before I died.
I hear the milkman setting the clinking bottles down outside.

MIDTERM ELECTION RESULTS, 2010

My old buddy, my body!
What happened to drive us apart?
Think of our trips to Bologna.
Think of our Ducati racebikes screaming.
We drank hypersonic grappa.

We got near the screaming Goyas.
What's blinding is Velázquez.
We never left the Prado—
And never saw Madrid!
That's what we did.

We met for lunch at the Paris Ritz.
We walked arm in arm
Through Place Vendôme.
Each put out a wrist
To try on a watch at Patek Philippe.

Unseparated Siamese twins,
We had to have the same girlfriend
And slept with her together.
We hopped on the Concorde,
Front cabin, seat 1.

Oh not to be meek and ache
And drop dead straining on the toilet seat.
Everyone on the sidewalk walks faster—
And didn't you use to walk
Springing up on the balls of your feet!

A single-engine light airplane
Snores in the slow blue dreamy afternoon.
This is our breakup.
We are down here falling apart.
The ocean crashes and crashes.

I put my arms around you—
But it's no good.
I climb the stairs—
It's not the same.
It's a flameout and windmill restart!

SNOW

Snow is what it does.
It falls and it stays and it goes.
It melts and it is here somewhere.
We all will get there.

CHARLIE

IN MEMORY OF CHARLES P. SIFTON (1935—2009)

I remember the judge in a particular
Light brown chalk-stripe suit
In which he looked like a boy,
Half hayseed, half long face, half wild horse on the plains,
Half the poet Boris Pasternak with a banjo pick,
Plucking a twanging banjo and singing Pete Seeger labor songs.

I remember a particular color of
American hair,
A kind of American original orange,
Except it was rather red, the dark colors of fire,
In a Tom Sawyer hairstyle,
Which I guess means naturally

Unjudicial and in a boyish
Will Rogers waterfall
Over the forehead,
And then we both got bald . . .
My Harvard roommate, part of my heart,
The Honorable Charles Proctor Sifton of the Eastern District.

Charlie,
Harvard sweet-talked you and me into living in Claverly
Sophomore year, where no one wanted to be.
We were the elect, stars in our class selected
To try to make this palace for losers respected.
The privileged would light the working fireplaces of the rejected.

Everyone called you Tony except me, and finally—
After years—you told me you had put up with years of "Charlie"
From me, but it had been hard!
Yes, but when now
I made an effort to call you Tony, it sounded so odd to you,
You begged me to come back home. Your Honor,

The women firefighters you ruled in favor of lift their hoses high,
Lift their hoses high,
Like elephants raising their trunks trumpeting.
Flame will never be the same. Sifton, row the boat ashore.
Then you'll hear the trumpet blow.
Hallelujah!

Then you'll hear the trumpet sound.
Trumpet sound
The world around.
Flame will never be the same!
Sifton, row the boat ashore.
Tony and Charlie is walking through that door.

ARNOLD TOYNBEE, MAC BUNDY,
HERCULES BELLVILLE

Seventy-two hours literally without sleep.
Don't ask.
I found myself standing at the back
Of Sanders Theatre
For a lecture by Arnold Toynbee.

Standing room only.
Oxford had just published
With great fanfare Volume X of his interminable
Magnum opus, *A Study of History*.
McGeorge Bundy, the dean of the faculty,

Later JFK's
National Security Adviser, then LBJ's, came out onstage
To invite all those standing in the back
To come up onstage and use
The dozen rows of folding chairs already

Set out for the Harvard Choral Society
Performance the next day.
Bundy was the extreme of Brahmin excellence.
I floated up there in a trance.
His penis was a frosted cocktail shaker pouring out a cocktail,

But out came jellied napalm.
The best and the brightest
Drank the fairy tale.
The Groton School and Skull and Bones plucked his lyre.
Hercules Bellville died today.

He apparently said to friends:
"Tut, tut, no long faces now."
He got married on his deathbed,
Having set one condition for the little ceremony: no hats.
I knew I would lapse

Into a coma in full view of the Harvard audience.
I would struggle to stay awake
And start to fall asleep.
I would jerk awake in my chair
And almost fall on the floor. I put Hercky

In a poem of mine called "Fucking" thirty-one years ago, only
I called him Pericles in my poem.
At the end of "Fucking," as he had in life,
Hercules pulled out a sterling silver–plated revolver
At a dinner party in London,

And pointed it at people, who smiled.
I had fallen in love at first sight
With a woman there I was about to meet.
One didn't know if the thing could be fired.
That was the poem.

NICE WEATHER

This is what it's like at the end of the day.
But soon the day will go away.
Sunlight preoccupies the cross street.
It and night soon will meet.
Meanwhile, there is Central Park.
Now the park is getting dark.

LONDON

The woman who's dying is trying to lose her life.
It's a great adventure
For everyone trying to help her.
Actually, death avoids her, doesn't want to hurt her.

So to speak, opens her hand and gently takes away the knife
Everyone well-meaning wants her to use on herself.
There is no knife, of course.
And she's too weak.

If you're too ill, the clinic near Zurich that helps
People leave this world won't.
If you're that medicated and out of it and desperate,
You may not be thinking right about wanting to end your life.

If you're near death, you may be *too* near
For the clinic to help you over the barrier.
She weakly screams she wants to die.
Hard to believe her pain is beyond the reach of drugs.

Please die. Please do. Her daughters don't want her to die and do.
The world of dew is a world of dew and yet
What airline will fly someone this sick?
They can afford a hospital plane but

Can she still swallow? The famous barbiturate cocktail
The clinic is licensed to administer isn't the Fountain of Youth.
But what if she gets there and drinks it and it only makes her ill?
And she vomits? It's unreal.

MOUNT STREET GARDENS

I'm talking about Mount Street.
Jackhammers give it the staggers.
They're tearing up dear Mount Street.
It's got a torn-up face like Mick Jagger's.

I mean, this is Mount Street!
Scott's restaurant, the choicest oysters, brilliant fish;
Purdey, the great shotgun maker—the street is complete
Posh plush and (except for Marc Jacobs) so English.

Remember the old Mount Street,
The quiet that perfumed the air
Like a flowering tree and smelled sweet
As only money can smell, because after all this was Mayfair?

One used to stay at the Connaught
Till they closed it for a makeover.
One was distraught
To see the dark wood brightened and sleekness take over.

Designer grease
Will help guests slide right into the zone.
Prince Charles and his design police
Are tickled pink because it doesn't threaten the throne.

I exaggerate for effect—
But isn't it grand, the stink of the stank,
That no sooner had the redone hotel just about got itself perfect
Than the local council decided: new street, new sidewalk, relocate the taxi rank!

Turn away from your life—away from the noise!—
Leaving the Connaught and Carlos Place behind.
Hidden away behind those redbrick buildings across the street are serious joys:
Green grandeur on a small enough scale to soothe your mind,

And birdsong as liquid as life was before you were born.
Whenever I'm in London I stop by this delightful garden to hear
The breeze in the palatial trees blow its shepherd's horn.
I sit on a bench in Mount Street Gardens and London is nowhere near.

ONE LAST KICK FOR DICK

IN MEMORY OF RICHARD POIRIER (1925—2009)

Old age is not for sissies but death is just disgusting.
It's a dog covering a bitch, looking so serious, looking ridiculous, thrusting.
The EMS team forces a tube down your airway where blood is crusting.
Imagine internal organs full of gravel oozing and rusting.
An ancient vase crossing the street on a walker, trudgingly trusting
The red light won't turn green, falls right at the cut in the curb, bursting, busting.
You're your ass covered with dust that your dust mop was sick of dusting.
The windshield wipers can't keep up. The wind is gusting.
A massive hemorrhagic bleed in the brain stem is Emerson readjusting.

Why did the fucker keep falling?
I'm calling you. Why don't you hear me calling?
Why did his faculties keep failing?
I'm doing my usual shtick with him and ranting and railing.
You finally knocked yourself unconscious and into the next world
Where Ralph Waldo Emerson, in the ballroom of the mind, whirled and twirled.
Fifty-three years ago, at the Ritz in Boston, we tried one tutorial session in the bar.
You got so angry you kicked me under the table. Our martinis turned black as tar.
And all because your tutee told you Shakespeare was overrated. I went too far.

From

*Widening Income
Inequality*

(2016)

REMEMBERING ELAINE'S

We drank our faces off until the sun arrived,
Night after night, and most of us survived
To waft outside to sunrise on Second Avenue,
And felt a kind of Wordsworth wonderment—the morning new,
The sidewalk fresh as morning dew—and us new, too.

How wonderful to be so magnified.
Every Scotch and soda had been usefully applied.
You were who you weren't till now.
We'd been white Harvard piglets sucking on the whisky sow
And now we'd write a book, without having to know how.

If you didn't get a hangover, that was one kind of bad
And was a sign of something, but if you had
Tranquilizers to protect yourself before you went to work,
Say as a doctor interning at nearby New York Hospital, don't be a jerk,
Take them, take loads of them, and share them, and don't smirk.

We smoked Kools, unfiltered Camels, and papier maïs Gitanes,
The fat ones Belmondo smoked in *Breathless*—and so did Don,
Elaine's original red-haired cokehead maître d'
Who had a beautiful wife, dangerously.
But stay away from the beautiful wife or else catastrophe.

Many distinguished dead were there
At one of the front tables, fragrant talk everywhere.
Plimpton, Mailer, Styron, Bobby Short—fellows, have another drink.
You had to keep drinking or you'd sink.
Smoking fifty cigarettes a day made your squid-ink fingers stink.

Unlucky people born with the alcoholic gene
Were likely to become alcoholics. Life is mean
That way, because others who drank as much or more didn't
Succumb, but just kept on drinking—and didn't
Do cocaine, and didn't get fucked up, and just didn't!

The dead are gone—
Their thousand and one nights vanished into dawn.
Were they nothing but tubs of guts, suitably gowned, waiting around
Till dawn turned into day? *Last round!*
Construction of the new Second Avenue subway enters the ground.

Aldrich once protested to Elaine that his bill for the night was too high.
She showed him his tab was for seventeen Scotches and he started to cry.
(Or was it eighteen?)
We were the scene.
Now the floor has been swept clean.

Everyone's gone.
Elaine and Elaine's have vanished into the dawn.
Elaine the woman, who weighed hundreds of pounds, is floating around—
Her ghost calls out: *Last round!*
Wailing, construction of the new Second Avenue subway pounds the ground.

CITY

Right now, a dog tied up in the street is barking
With the grief of being left,
A dog bereft.
Right now, a car is parking.

The dog emits
Petals of a barking flower and barking flakes of snow
That float upward from the street below
To where another victim sits:

Who listens to the whole city
And the dog honking like a car alarm,
And doesn't mean the dog any harm,
And doesn't feel any pity.

FRANCE NOW

I slide my swastika into your lubricious Place Clichy.
I like my women horizontal and when they stand up vicious and Vichy.
I want to jackboot rhythmically down your Champs-Élysées
With my behind behind me taking selfies of the Grand Palais.
Look at my arm raised in the razor salute of greeting.
I greet you like a Caesar, *Heil!* for our big meeting.
My open-top Mercedes creeps through the charming, cheering crowd.
I greet you, lovely body of Paris, you who are so proud,
And surtout you French artists and French movie stars who
Are eager to collaborate and would never hide a Jew.

My oh my. How times have changed.
But the fanatics have gotten even more deranged.
Seventy-five years after Hitler toured charming, cheering Paris, Parisians say
They won't give in to terrorist tyranny, and yesterday
Two million people marched arm in arm, hand in hand,
After the latest murderous horror, to take a stand
Against the fascist Nazi Islamist jihadi blasphemous horror and murder.
Absurd is getting absurder.
It's absurd in France to be a Jew
Because someone will want to murder you—

Someone who spreads infidel blood all over the walls and floor like jam—
Someone who, like you, doesn't eat ham.
He/she activates her/his suicide vest.
Children just out of the nest
Wearing a suicide vest
Are the best.
It's alarming
And queer to read Osama bin Laden writing an essay about global warming.
So he was also human, like the ISIS fighters writing
Poems in the manner of the great pre-Islamic odes in the midst of the fighting.

We are the Marseillaise. We are la civilisation française. Make no mistake,
Civilization is at stake.
We are a paper frigate sailing on a burning lake—
Many decks and sails, and white and fancy as a wedding cake.
Listen. The Mu'allaqa of Imru' al-Qays, the *Iliad* of the Arabs, keeps singing
In the desert, "Come, let us weep," while the bells of Notre-Dame keep ringing
With alarm. In one of the Hadith,
Muhammad crowns me with a wreath
But damns me for eternity, Imru' al-Qays, and Labīd as well,
But me especially as the most poetic of poets and their leader into hell.

ROBESPIERRE

Who wouldn't like to have the power to kill
Friends and enemies at will and fill
The jails with people you don't know or know
Only slightly from meeting them a year ago,
Maybe at an AA meeting, where they don't even use last names.
Hi, I'm Fred. Instead of being someone who constantly blames
And complains, why not annihilate?
Why not hate? Why not exterminate? Why not violate
Their rights and their bodies? Tell
The truth. Who wouldn't like to? There's a wishing well in hell
Where every wish is granted.
Decapitation gets decanted.
Suppose you have the chance
To guillotine the executioner after having guillotined everyone else in France?

A PROBLEM WITH THE LANDING GEAR

Cars traveling the other way
On the other side of the double yellow dividing line
Carry people you don't know and never will.
The woman on the other side of the bed reading a book
Is likewise going somewhere else.

You are and you aren't yours.
It's like you're on the other side of the road
From yourself in your car.
You're on the other side of the bed
From her book.

AUTUMN LEAVES

Plop the live lobster into boiling water and let it scream.
You both turn red.
Of course you have to eat it dead.
There can be unfertilized roe
That will turn red also, maliciously delicious, called coral.
The colder the ocean waters the lobster came from, the sweeter
The meat boiled in the brain of heat.
The lobster at the end is as incontinent as falling leaves and doesn't know.

It's agony to be turning into something else—
And when you certainly weren't intending to.
This room must be the bedroom, but it smells.
A mouse still alive is standing on the trap, stuck in glue,
Like a man trapped standing on the roof of his submerged car,
Or a woman making love to herself seated in front of a mirror.
Little shrieks from you as you try to get unstuck from you
Becomes a raving hippopotamus that sings and sobs.

The fuel for this ravisher unicycle of a world,
Going faster and faster, ever more horsepower,
Is not the president of the United States anymore.
The man on the roof of the car waves his arms.
The butterfly in love lands on fresh tar, tacky goo.
I'm turning into something I wasn't intending to be—
In agony after the awful metamorphosis
Into a suddenly human being.

It's so fascinating to watch a woman masturbating.
It makes your eyes turn blue.
You watch her doing it for you.
She's watching, too.
You realize it's true.
She's doing it for you.
The man's cell phone is soaked.
He's stuck on top of his submerged SUV yelling into the vast.

The new Swatch wristwatch on my wrist
Handcuffs the suspect for having sexual intercourse
With someone much younger, twisting in the noose.
Let them dangle and twist.
It's agony turning into something else.
Some sort of cockroach that smells slightly rotten
Walks around on hairs for legs and mutters something,
Then puts on a fine suit and goes outside.

Outside it's fall. This is the weather that people like,
Perfect for people who hate the heat.
The sun shines down at a different angle
Through the atmosphere, producing that look, that light.
A first responder is coming with a boat
To rescue the man from the roof of his car, a helicopter lowers a ladder
To the boiling lobster. Let me explain to you something
I've never understood.

THE BIRD ON THE CROCODILE'S BACK

The man can't stay awake. He falls asleep.
It's noon, it's afternoon, repeatedly he falls in deep,
Seated at his desk or in an armchair, as if to try to write a poem meant
A flash flood of sleep and drowning on Parnassus in his tent,
Or something else equally not good.
The guy's completely gone and sawing wood,
Snoring and snorting—until one snort wakes him—
And where is he? he can't think where he is—which shakes him.

He's upside down and he can see
The parachute he's hanging from is tangled high up in a tree.
He passes out again and drools.
This apparently is one of the Muse's rules.
He hears the pleasant droning of the plane he jumped from flying away,
But he's in his study and it's the same day.
He's in his study now and here's his long-dead dog.
Jimmy, my sweety boy, my Jimmy, come back to me through the fog.

Musa, mihi causas memora . . . you know?
You've seen a baby lift its foot to suck its toe
And then go back to sleep for several years
And then wake up to find a whole nation in tears . . .
Multiple assassinations, black and white, white and black,
Chest covered with medals split open by a national heart attack.
Baby has grown up to be an outrage carrying a weapon.
He's graduated from West Point and found little babies to step on.

Liquid gold streams down the buildings all the way down Broadway
At sunset, after a perfect fall day in May, the sky so blue it made you say
Something had to be God to lead to this
Furious brilliance you wouldn't want to miss
By being dead, for example, or otherwise asleep.
He saw a man once start to weep
But stop himself in time,
Because crying for a certain sort of man is correctly considered a crime.

Look how the sky is turning beautiful black and blue,
Reminding us how the aftermath of pain can be beautiful and true.
The apartment lights before they go out come on.
Hours later it's dawn.
Narcolepsy is supposed to be the subject, but it really isn't the subject, nor
Is the man fleeing from a crime he committed in Ulan Bator.
He didn't cry in the hotel elevator.
He's not the Ulan Bator crying elevator satyr.

That didn't stop the girl with the eating disorder driving the car from crashing.
He comes to after the crash, as usual at his desk, splashing
His face with cold water from the nearby lake,
Though he's already thinking of the next move to make.
He'll move to Rio. He'll move to Napoli. He opens the study door.
He'll move to the little apartment on the second floor.
Every day alive is dawn.
The lights before they go out go on.

THE LOVELY REDHEAD

In the colored section of St. Louis, back
When life was white and black,
I'm skimming the modest rooftops in a stolen black Cadillac,
Which happens to be my father's, and I fly too high,
And wake up in my bed this morning wondering why
I'm an old white man in bed in 2012 in Manhattan
Not next to a lovely redhead whose skin is satin.
Pardon me if I grab the remote before I open my eyes.
They're going to televise
One World Trade Center's rise
While the Empire State Building stands there and practically dies
And the Chrysler Building cries.
The tallest building in the world this morning is Dubai's.
Get over it, guys. Say your goodbyes.

Jabbering jackhammers talk their way into my teeth
As I exit from my dentist's office.
Every street in New York, it seems, is being dug up.
Every day in New York flaps like a stork over streets
Giving birth. Almost every building in Manhattan
Is swaddled with scaffolding while inspectors check
For stuff that might fall off. Incidents
Involving some poor schmuck
On the sidewalk getting smushed lead to city contracts.
Somebody the city likes
Is making big bucks. This is about a smartphone
Surrounded by so much noise
It isn't able to.
No one is getting out of this alive.

No one was celebrating noise
Until the great homosexual American composer John Cage
Discovered the great American sound of road rage,
But with no automobile involvement, and lots of silence.
It's the roar of a subway car
Filled with silent New Yorkers silently snapping their fingers
To the beat coming out of an earbud in one ear,
And music they're hearing that we the audience can't hear.
They rise from their seats all at once and start to dance.
Music turns people into this and
Noise keeps turning into New York.
A drive-by-shooting shout is rap, the rhyming slave-rebellion app.
I sing of noise.
I sing in praise.

The greatest city in the world is like
The prostate in a normally aging man,
Constantly enlarging in some new direction.
The metropolitan prostate
Continues to grow, which to be sure can block the flow.
As soon as a funky neighborhood starts to grow and glow,
The real estate developers move in and really annoy.
They slaughter buildings like livestock.
But good things happen nevertheless.
The Meatpacking District is only the latest.
The Red Rooster restaurant in Harlem is so chic.
Let's sneak a peek.
In summer, there are tables outside.
Blacks and whites, young and old, eat side by side.

This has been the warmest Manhattan
Since temperatures have been recorded,
And the Hudson and the East River continue to rise,
Along with the civilization they are part of—
And the rents in the East Village,
And the number of restaurants.
This island is a toupee
Of towers, floating away.
Don't drown in your rivers, not yet.
Maybe five hundred years from now, not now.
My smartphone works in the noise but can't hear,
But doesn't want to be anywhere but here. What a shock!
Or as they used to mock in the Manhattan D.A.'s Office,
No shit, Sherlock!

A crocodile twenty feet long at least,
With a human leg and foot sticking out of its mouth,
Is basking in the sun in Bryant Park
Right behind the New York Public Library.
I was coming out of the dentist's office on Fifty-fifth near Fifth.
I am always.
I have a call coming in on the other line—
Let me put you on hold.
This is he. I can't hear you.
Inside the nearby Museum of Modern Art (MoMA),
The curators are in an induced coma.
The digestive pleasure a crocodile feels is great.
It makes the eaten person sort of swoon.
It makes for quite an afternoon.

I'd rather talk about the weather.
I'd rather talk about which airlines I prefer.
I'd rather talk about my periodontist and my MacBook Air.
Don't try to talk to me about Guillaume Apollinaire.
Laugh at me if you like, but actually it's sad.
You people who know, know love is brief and being old is bad,
Know tribal wars devour the world, and little children are starving.
Five million orphans in Ethiopia aren't riding
Beautiful Italian racing motorcycles to outrun their problem.
Chemotherapy is as brutal as the cancers it doesn't cure.
Starving children get that look.
I'd rather talk about my London tailor.
I'd rather talk about who makes the lightest luggage with wheels.
The best luggage these days glides along on grease.

Look at me, whizzing through airport security,
A privileged man, a certain age, some hair left,
Taking off my shoes, folding my coat and placing it in a plastic tray,
Computer, wallet, taking my belt off,
Having traveled far and wide, having lived through wars
Without once fighting, having read through libraries
In order to board the flight from here to get
To there. The struggle to leave is futile but
The arrival will be meaningful. Leaving museums behind,
I'm in the security line behind a lovely redhead as she undresses
With me for the X-ray. Let her red hair stand
For everything life is worth.
Her loveliness charms the alarms,
But will the weeds and the wars wilt and wither all around the earth?

I'm on the High Line, goodbye, which in a previous life
Was the elevated railroad track along the Hudson, goodbye,
Brought back to life as a walkway and park to rewrite in.
I'm rewriting my life to make it less accessible, goodbye,
And the parts that rhyme
I'll bury in lime.
In the street below, but a block away,
Diane von Furstenberg's stylish wrap dresses are on display.
Who, five hundred years from now, will care or know
About the Meatpacking District or DVF Studio?
The city is dying and living, farewell,
Along with the civilization it is part of,
And which Diane von Furstenberg is part of the art of,
Once upon a time, long, long ago.

MAN IN SLICKER

A man is talking to himself again.
He strolls down Broadway in the rain.
He's hidden in a slicker, so he's yellow, obvious.
A rainy day on Broadway looks like Auschwitz, more or less.
He has a fancy accent so he isn't Jewish, is he?

He walks down Piccadilly, more or less.
Not exactly talking to himself, more like quiet shouting.
He's a hotdog wearing yellow mustard spouting
A fancy accent but he isn't English.
In fact, he'd sink England in the North Atlantic with relish.

Down to Eighty-second Street and back each day,
Ten blocks or sometimes more each way.
Like waking from a dream and you realize you're shouting.
But you're happy and you're walking.
I'm quite aware I'm making faces.

I'll look good in my black chalk-stripe suit,
Savile Row astride a red Ducati racer
For a fashion magazine, a fancy joke
Done morbidly, my tongue sticking out like I'm dead.
What if they remove my tongue from my head?

Talking, talking, talking, at my desk, in silence,
Putting my head in the open mouth of my MacBook Air.
Being alive is served to the keyboard raw or rare.
The poem eats anything, doesn't care.
I sing of Obama's graying second-term hair.

It's me—I'm talking to myself again.
I'm walking down to Eighty-second Street
To Barnes & Noble to buy my own book. Blue sky. Summer day.
The Broadway center strip of bushy trees
Is a green fluorescence in the summer breeze.

Let the homeless pick through the trash—
It's a heavenly day in heaven nonetheless!
I find filth to eat and I beg—
And pretend I'm the Shah of Iran.
Anything but I mean *anything* to sing you a Broadway song!

I'm talking on my cell to Galassi on his—
We're lepidoptera fluttering our way to a matinée at the opera.
It's a drastic new *Don Giovanni*.
An absolute swine gloriously sings to his harem of flowers for hours
And asks, Who has a more beautiful name than Mitzi Angel?

We dine, sipping flowers and wine.
Winged butterflies of refinement, each on an assignment.
Galassi's is to inhale Montale and Leopardi
And cross-pollinate the language of the tribe.
Mine's harder to describe.

THE END OF SUMMER

I'm from St. Louis and Budweiser.
I'm from the Seidel Coal and Coke Company and the Mississippi.
I'm from the old streets near Forest Park,
And T. S. Eliot, and the B-movie actress Virginia Mayo.

My mother thought she was the daughter of Helen Traubel,
The vast Wagnerian soprano born in St. Louis,
And thought J. Edgar Hoover, head of the FBI, was probably her father.
I'm from Stan Musial and the Brown Shoe Company.

I remember the brick alleys behind the massive houses.
Palaces and their stables (turned into garages) lined the outside of a long oval.
At each end was a turreted guardhouse above the iron gates.
These were the famous St. Louis private streets.

Imagine freestanding Florentine palazzi on little American plots,
Complete with rusticated masonry and brutal grandeur.
H. H. Richardson, the designer of Harvard's Sever Hall,
Designed one of them, forty-seven rooms in all, hardly small.

Vandeventer Place and Portland Place and Westmoreland.
The Congress Hotel and the Senate Apartments.
Lindbergh's medals were on display nearby on Lindell Boulevard.
I could climb down an embankment and play on the train tracks.

Where demolished Vandeventer Place once stood,
Stone magnificence where Teddy Roosevelt once stayed,
Was not that far from demolished Kiel Opera House, where
Mother took me to hear Traubel with the visiting Metropolitan Opera.

My father had a season box at the outdoor Muny Opera.

My father had a cop he paid who parked our car there.

The 1904 World's Fair was in the magical Forest Park night air.

I hear crickets singing in the dark sweet Missouri heat their insolent despair.

KARL

IN MEMORY OF KARL MILLER (1931–2014)

The trees are waving their arms around
Like some ridiculous performance of modern dance.
They look like ludicrous John Hollander raving about the excellence
Of late Auden. Stop this nonsense! You're not dancers!
At Ninety-second and Broadway, I'm afraid that's
What it looks like they think they are.

We had droll things to say about everything we liked or didn't.
And weren't we clever and didn't we have fun!
We said everything we had to say
Until the plane ran out of runway,
Took off while it was landing—and you were gone.
Such suffering and sickness and sweet good times!

I see a rainbow above a lawn being watered,
Dragonfly iridescence, hissing sprayer-mist, quiet—
And hear the deafening roar of Niagara Falls—
And smell the dainty rain about to fall.
The shower head is the entire sky!
Jihadi extremists

Will want to behead the shower head
For showering us with delights and letting us do our work.
The plane is about to take off
And at the same time is about to land. Bring back those days
When I complained that your smart-set English (Scottish) thing
Was to mock a friend the minute he left the room!

You've left the room. I will not see my darling dear again,
Which is what I'll call this poem
Written to remember Karl Miller, who has died in London.
I shall not look upon his like again.
I send this teeny, tiny rescue flare into the universe
As things on planet Earth get worse.

SUNSET AT SWAN LAKE

> *My little girl is singing: Ah! Ah! Ah! Ah! I do not understand the*
> *meaning of this, but I feel its meaning. She wants to say that everything*
> *Ah! Ah! is not horror but joy.*
> —Nijinsky's *Diary*

Nijinsky wants to be Nijinsky's body double. Nijinsky wants to splash in puddles.
He wants to rip the roof off and let the rain in and Ukraine in and be sane in.
Diaghilev and the rest of our kindergarten class will get soaked.
Windows and windshields—do you understand it's raining!
Headlights on in the daytime in the May warm rain
And lights on sweetly in the darkened living room
Feels like what it feels like staying home,
The music turned down low and cars hissing through the pain.
God asks the mirror: "I don't have the emotional depth other people do, do you?"
He never wanted to, though he wanted to.
God stares into the full-length mirror in the foyer—
The border guard at the checkpoint stares back.
The guard won't let him enter the mirror.
"I only have one feeling and you've hurt my feeling!"

POLIO DAYS

Why did they send us to summer camp—were they being parental?
Swimming pools—any gathering place—were considered plague central.
Everywhere you went, billboards displayed the smiling faces
March of Dimes kids offered up to go with their metal leg braces.

Imagine being inside an iron lung and having to swallow the rotten truth
That life was going to be one long bad connection inside a telephone booth,
And that you'd been really unlucky and would never walk
Because it had happened before there was vaccine from Jonas Salk.

Truman was in the White House but polio was the president
In the years of the plague, when our American atom bombs were pubescent.
The milkman delivered the milk in unsterilized glass bottles.
Aunt Edna served home-killed fried chicken, wobbling her wattles.

I can't imagine it. Imagine being stuck
Inside an iron lung and not being able to touch your genitals or fuck—
Forever—for the length of your brief stay here on earth,
In a death train's sleeping car's shut-tight upper berth.

Meanwhile, the scenery of cities and countryside flashes past outside.
The tickety-tock of the train on the tracks is the groom and the bride
Making love in your brain rhythmically, or is it the air-pump breathing you?
Breathing is all you will ever do. That isn't true—

You will write symphonies. You will sing *Leaves of Grass*.
You will jump higher than Nijinsky and smirk at him, Kiss my ass!
You will sit down at your desk right now and watch the snow
Falling in a million white pieces, and say hello.

ME

The fellow talking to himself is me,
Though I don't know it. That's to say, I see
Him every morning shave and comb his hair
And then lose track of him until he starts to care,
Inflating sex dolls out of thin air
In front of his computer, in a battered leather chair
That needs to be thrown out . . . then I lose track
Until he strides along the sidewalk on the attack
With racist, sexist outbursts. What a treat
This guy is, glaring at strangers in the street!
Completely crazy but not at all insane.
He's hot but there's frostbite in his brain.
He's hot but freezing cold, and oh so cool.
He's been called a marvelously elegant ghoul.

But with a torn rotator cuff, even an elegant fawn
Has to go through shoulder seizures to get his jacket on.
He manages spastically. His left shoulder's gone.
It means, in pain, he's drastically awake at dawn.
A friend of his with pancreatic cancer, who will die,
Is not in pain so far, and she will try
To palliate her death, is what her life is now.
The fellow's thinking to himself, Yes but how?
Riding a motorcycle very fast is one way to.
The moon and stars rapidly enter you
While you excrete the sun. You ride across the earth
Looking for a place to lay the eggs of your rebirth.
The eggs crack open and out comes everyone.
The chicks chirp, and it's begun, and it's fun.

You keep on writing till you write yourself away,
And even after—when you're nothing—you still stay.
The eggs crack open and out comes everyone.
The chicks chirp, the poems speak—and it's again begun!
Speaking of someone else for a change, not me,
There was that time in Stockholm when, so strangely,
Outside a restaurant, in blinding daylight, a tiny bird
Circled forever around us and then without a word
Lightly, lightly landed on my head and settled there
And you burst into tears. I was unaware
That ten years before the same thing had happened just
After your young daughter died and now it must
Have been Maria come back from the dead a second time to speak
And receive the recognition we all seek.

WIDENING INCOME INEQUALITY

I live a life of appetite and, yes, that's right,
I live a life of privilege in New York,
Eating buttered toast in bed with cunty fingers on Sunday morning.
Say that again?
I have a rule—
I never give to beggars in the street who hold their hands out.

I woke up this morning in my air-conditioning.
At the end of my legs were my feet.
Foot and foot stretched out outside the duvet looking for me!
Get up. Giddyup. Get going.
My feet were there on the far side of my legs.
Get up. Giddyup. Get going.

I don't really think I am going to.
Obama is doing just fine.
I don't think I'm going to.
Get up. Giddyup. Get going.
I can see out the window it isn't raining.
So much for the endless forecasts, always wrong.

The poor are poorer than they ever were.
The rich are richer than the poor.
Is it true about the poor?
It's always possible to be amusing.
I saw a rat down in the subway.
So what if you saw a rat.

I admire the poor profusely.
I want their autograph.
They make me shy.
I keep my distance.
I'm getting to the bottom of the island.
Lower Broadway comes to a boil and City Hall is boiling.

I'm half asleep but I'm awake.
At the other end of me are my feet
In shoes of considerable sophistication
Walking down Broadway in the heat.
I'm half asleep in the heat.
I'm, so to speak, wearing a hat.

I'm no Saint Francis.
I'm in one of my trances.
When I look in a mirror,
There's an old man in a trance.
There's a Gobi Desert,
And that's poetry, or rather rhetoric.

You see what happens if you don't make sense?
It only makes sense to not.
You feel the flicker of a hummingbird
It takes a second to find.
You hear a whirr.
It's here. It's there. It hovers, begging, hand out.

One lives a life of appetite and, yes,
Lives a life of privilege in New York.
So many wretched refuse with their hands out.
Help me please get something to eat.
I'm a pope in a pulpit of air-conditioned humility
And widening income inequality, eating mostly pussy.

A lady-in-waiting at the imperial court
Flutters her fan in the Heian (Kyoto) heat.
How delicately she does it.
You can't see
How you want to live?
She perspires only a bit.

Outside the Department of Motor Vehicles palace, Francis of Assisi
Is eating garbage with the homeless
And writing a poem to God,
And to our lord Brother Sun.
Never mind that the sun is dangerously hot
Out on the sidewalk.

Open your arms like a fresh pack of cards
And shuffle the deck.
Now open your heart.
Now open your art.
Now get down on your knees in the street
And eat.

From

Peaches Goes It Alone

(2018)

ATHENA

Your favorites are the polar bears
Who these days have to walk on snot,
Global warming underfoot.
Snot, not snow, is now their natural habitat with climate change
And oceans rising.
The polar bears are doomed and ask you why.

The humid New York City that your arms are spread above
Like wings before you fly
To some new fantasy of yours of Mediterranean
Family happiness, which of course turns out to be
Passionately Greek tragedy pouring
Blue sky into dark clouds and it will storm.
The humid city opens up its heart
To yours.
What's needed is relief and a release
From.

Never mind your horrible claustrophobia
In the subway in from Astoria—
Never mind that there's Attic
Atavistic sibling rivalry at home—and a queen who's unkind.
Never mind.
And dad the king always off upstate hunting.
Greek America. These vulgar bejeweled peasants are kings and gods.

But what's with this heat wave! Are you in love?

Shudders of lightning and the smell of burning hair.
Electric magic in the sullen New York air.
Heat so intense even the cockroaches seek shelter.
This ultimate heat wave will abolish everything but air-conditioning
And evil and the fear of flying.

You're afraid of flying but you've made up your mind to fly.
You're afraid that all the passengers on the planet will die.
Your determination makes the Hudson River wink
As you rise wheels-up at long last to
Indomitable.

A sky of melting icebergs will rain down on Manhattan
When your plane lands safely back from Greece and your Greek cousins—
Back from Greek politics and debt and the unglued European Union.
The tires touch down on the New World tarmac and *squeal*
And all the plane applauds,
And your dreadful sister mocks,
Because you've almost overcome your fears . . .

The rain will bring relief to what
Your open arms are raised above, the way
The outstretched arms of Christ bless Rio,
Protect the poor and the police in the favelas,
Allow the Olympics to unspool its glories.

Hot rain is fatly splatting down
On Freedom Tower downtown.
Freedom Tower downtown goes up and up.
The hot hiss of hate turns to a hush.
Don't stop now, dearest, help us, don't stop.
The air is fresh. The rain has stopped.

Life isn't mostly Mozart,
But Mozart is a start, plays a part, as does all great art.

Late that night, in Lincoln Center's outdoor plaza,
After hours of tears, your heart burst into stars.

Your beautiful dark hair is not quite black, Athena.
Your beautiful smile is not quite meek, goddess.

Save us.

TOO MUCH

When even getting a haircut seems too much,
And trimming your toenails and fingernails takes too much strength,
When more than you have is what's required,
At least that's what you think,
And even the thought of reading a book makes you tired,
Then it's time to get on your motorcycle and ride far out to sea
And run out of money and blink S.O.S. and sink.

I was once in love myself.
I loved politics in those days as well.
Now I stare up at the sun.
I stretch out on the sidewalk under the moon
And greet each day as an adversary.
I thought I knew everything, then I met you.
It's rather like how a bald man once was hairy.

Everyone should be an optimist, of course.
Have the experience of marriage so you can have the experience of a divorce.
Sing, or rather scream, until you're hoarse.
Actually, you're acting like a baby.
You don't mean anything you're saying
When you're the middle of a volcano
And your lava starts to flow.

Actually, I'm screaming like a baby for a breast or the bottle,
Maybe a bottle of red, either Italian or French.
I'll get a haircut.
I'll cut my toenails. What's come over me?
I'm ready to fall in love with life.
I'm ready to drink her pee.
I'll take a shower after.

I'm ready to travel the world
Except I've already been.
Cape Coast Castle in Ghana
Is literally whitewashed white.
The building moans like a ghost under the enormous African sun.
The dungeon holding pen for slaves is a sacred place.
At the so-called Door of No Return, tourist African-Americans pose.

Triste Afrique!
Every single African head of state is corrupt.
Yesterday I was francophone and snowing, today I'm July.
I hear the whine of the mosquitoes.
They land on their oil rig of legs and drill down.
They're sort of our nurses
In the form of a proboscis of six hollow needles drawing blood.

I fell in love once and then it was over.
I found a long dark hair of hers long after.
I believe in the power of love to enslave.
Oxygen enters a vacuum of not and explodes.
Our slave ships unload us on the dock,
Prodrome of everything to come.
Too much is often enough. Too much is almost enough.

THE EZRA POUND LOOK-ALIKE

It's always the same man
Who looks like Ezra Pound
Stretched out on the sidewalk
In front of Victoria's Secret.

No one knows what to make of his catastrophe.
What's it like to be Pound's look-alike?
Every day he pulls New York City
Over himself like a blanket and sleeps.

The sidewalk is a stairway to paradise
Down Broadway to the open road.
The possibilities ahead turn around and beckon.
A woman is marvelously shaking the tambourine.

Each slab of cement has its own story.
Don't step on the sidewalk cracks or do.
Everything is magical.
Things are about to happen.

The pitter-patter of a police helicopter overhead
Looking for you
In the streets below
Says it is beautiful but also it is true.

So when America is over,
What is there after?
There's more America, comerado!
There's always more.

Canoeing in northern Canada
Where wolves howl in the night,
And then rain tries to tear your tent apart,
Is just the same as Manhattan.

How sweet when you're American
To hear how grown-up you are
From the lady tousling your hair
Who can't see into your brain.

She might as well be a high-rise in the clouds
Reaching down to pat your curls.
Your face is at the level of her thing
And will be for the rest of your life.

You're where babies come out
And you are young forever,
And grow up
Only so far.

You're green as a grasshopper, America,
And jump that high.
You were green as a salad recently,
Which means summer is ending.

The future isn't over,
Even for the people left out.
It used to be there was no place that wasn't
Your stepmother making you a pie.

MISS CHARLOTTE

Bring back the all-girls boarding schools for pedigreed girls
Where, morning and night, girls dressed and undressed.
Luxurious lawns and trees rode to hounds.
Horses the girls owned waited in padded stalls.

Think of the cold showers these aristocrats took.
Think of the dorm-room mirrors which sometimes saw
A cold girl lying on top of a warm girl
While a pretty girl with a pimply face on her bed on her back watched.

Have two rules, Miss Charlotte said:
Hard, good work and much fun.
She was addressing two favorites, Grits and little Bun-Bun.
There was gymkhana and dressage and raising the flag and French.

Keep up with the times, Miss Charlotte said. *Don't be narrow.*
Pile up on traditions and remember,
With God all things are possible.
On, on, with Foxcroft. Dare not let her die.

These ball gowns were tomboys who curtsy and bow.
These tigers were geldings life milks like a cow.
In life's cotillion, girls had to learn how
To be kapos at Dachau.

Kapos at Dachau, kapos at Dachau,
And pigeon-shooting on horseback at their plantations.
Once upon a time, Du Pont, Mellon, Frick, Whitney, Astor . . .
Astor was a disaster.

What got into Bun-Bun Astor
To make Miss Charlotte, who loved her, walk right past her?
Each child learned how to be her horse's master
And complete the dressage routine a little faster.

Night softly turns into light.
The gun Bun-Bun lifts out of her bra
Fires, blinding the room, flashing delight, killing Miss Charlotte outright.
Now the sun is fully up hurrah.

Miss Charlotte thought she heard a scream,
And woke from her dream.
Then began to weep.
Then went back to sleep.

AND NOW GOOD-MORROW
TO OUR WAKING SOULS

I wake each morning
To the sound of awful coughing
Coming from the street
Six floors below.
The same man sits there,
Wide awake at dawn,
On a narrow ledge, low to the sidewalk,
Barely wide enough
Not to cough and fall off.
The store he's outside is a Petco,
Closed of course at this hour,
Food and treats and toys for pets,
Leashes and collars
And bondage for dogs.
I wake early.
I let the light wake me.
I leave the bedroom curtains open
To have the light in the room.
From the bed, still in bed,
I listen to the coughing.
I walk over to the window.
The window is open
With the air conditioner on.
Time to be someone.
Time to put clothes on.
What have you done?
What will you do?
What will I do—what have I done!

IN LATE DECEMBER

FOR MITZI ANGEL

The man using the pay phone on Wall Street,
His back to you, is using it as a urinal,
And urinating—only logical!
Our degradation is complete.

The young woman, a crazy smile pickled in brine,
Cross-legged on the sidewalk in a T-shirt that says TOMORROW,
Holds a sign telling her sad story.
She's reading a paperback of *Lolita*, stealthily, behind the sign.

She could be you—
Stranger things have turned out to be true.
He could be me—
Don't rule out the possibility.

This shirtsleeves Christmas weather is lovely
And seriously weird.
El Niño is how Jesus was—
Both changed the climate.

Everyone will have a home. Everyone
Is safe and warm.
The homeless sleep on a bed of roses and sip ice wine (German *Eiswein*).
They spend their time deciding where they want to dine.

They spend the rest of their time thinking about the sublime
And exhuming corpses
So they don't have to beg for a living
From the living.

They bring back billions of bodies
And pile them in the apartment building lobbies
And repopulate the financial world with the dead
Like a dog bringing back a stick.

The stick is what was underground
Back in sunlight.
Cadavers and cremains hump on walkers down Wall Street
And a homeless hand reaches out to them for baksheesh.

She could be you!
Stranger things have turned out to be true.
He could be me—
I don't discount the possibility.

Jews, Christians, Muslims, others—it's Christmas morn.
Aloha, *amici*, Christ is born!
Flowers are fooled into thinking it's spring.
The little city birds sing.

ENGLAND NOW

FOR PAUL KEEGAN

I like to be dead.
That's what the dead say.

I'd rather be dead than so-called alive.
I like the lack of feeling.

But you know what?
That's the way I've always felt.

That's my way.
I'm feeling good.

I haven't been big on feeling.
I haven't been alive that much.

It rains all the time and it's cold in July.
Somewhere down south,

In the tropical humidity and heat
Of my brain below the belt,

Is where I vote.
I don't want any.

I eat what's there.
I don't import.

I am England
Under these newish circumstances.

A people who are proud to be dead said
So loud and clear.

GENERALISSIMO FRANCISCO FRANCO
IS STILL DEAD

Every time I sleep I leave a stain.
When I wake up, I climb out of a drain
And step into my feet and it is plain
That when I walk away I leave a lane
Of garbage on the carpet in the train.

Francisco Franco (El Caudillo) pokes his head up from the drain
Where he's been hiding with Saddam Hussein.
He waterboards the peasants with champagne.
Now maybe they'll vote to give this madly inane
Hitler buffoon his very own nuclear codes, let democracy reign!

Make Spain great again! I shouldn't touch it but I can't refrain
And don't restrain
Myself so what was once a tiny grain
Of pain
Is now a roaring lion with a mane.

Franco needs water for his golf courses so we can't complain
Out loud but it's insane—insane
Monsoons of rain
Drowning the automatic sprinkler systems that maintain
The greens, blinding windshields worldwide, Spain to Maine.

I can't stop rhyming! I can't. It's my domain!
Making more or less musical noise out of my fascist disdain.
I choose Francisco Franco, weakling strong man of Spain,
As my alter ego, bearer of my terror over what I can't attain
In the few years I have left, the minutes that remain . . .

Lacking tenderness, not something you can go to the store and obtain,
But which anyway does not pertain
To piloting an airplane
Dropping bombs on innocent civilians who remain
In pieces in the street under the boiling sun, Spaniards, pieces of Spain.

Don't drink and drive. Don't text while driving. Don't kill Lorca. Maintain
The good health of your car and tires and don't explain
To anyone when you're in the red-light district but remain
Alert also on the subway and don't feign
Ignorance because, though Franco is still dead, long may Franco reign!

DUCATI YEARS, DUCATI DAYS

I had a girlfriend who dumped me for a better job—
Which, frankly, made me laugh so hard I started to sob.

I'd been so disgustingly highfalutin—so grand!—ballooning on hot air
Above green pincushion fields with trees stuck in down there,

Snootily floating above and looking down,
My drinker's red nose tilted up arrogantly, red-nosed circus clown

Floating above life's road-rage-in-a-maze.
Ah, those were lovely Ducati years and Ducati days!

I rode my racers and felt superior.
Nothing could catch me—nothing inside me—just an exterior.

Almost all Ducati motorcycles in those fine days were red.
We Ducatisti rode red-hot Italian beauties on the track and in bed.

I squeeze into my old red race-team jacket to remember.
Rosso di competizione . . . but it's freezing December

Out on the street as I walk off last night's alcohol, ballooned in bulging down.
I'm the Michelin Man-Made-of-Tires, a clown

In down, tethered unsteadily to the ground,
With not too many more laps left to wobble around.

Skewered me like a kebab.
Left me for a better job.

EPITHALAMION FOR STEIN AND STEIN

Two hummingbirds visit the privet,
Flickering your eyes, drumming your heart,
Here and gone before you blink.
You walk airborne toward the start.

Fifteen minutes' drive to the beach and ocean,
Ten to Long Beach and the bay.
Jimmy the dog is asleep in a flower bed.
The sprinklers mist a rainbow in the Garden of Eden.

It's the hiss of the hose in the heat
Hosing down the sidewalk, fresh and neat,
And releasing the delicious odor of hot concrete.
It's dripping out of a swimming pool onto hot-under-your-feet.

You're a minute away from Main Street
And minutes away from the vulgar, sweet,
Tiny downtown, no bigger than a Twitter tweet,
And the American Hotel porch where you'll eat.

TO MAC GRISWOLD

Suddenly I'm ready to eat the world,
Starting with the food on my plate.
The waiter asks if everything's all right.
Everything's great.
Everything looks the same but nothingness is night.
Time to go back upstairs into more electric light.

My jaunty step is oral, enjoying everything.
This election year is the beginning.
The national falling apart will amount to something.
Suddenly I'm able to walk outside.
Suddenly I'm able to walk away.
Rain is falling on the other side of the street.

Thank you for the delicious food.
Thank you for my delicious mood.
It's time to get back upstairs and smirk and shirk work.
Writing poems is like being in Sing Sing singing.
It's like being a prisoner of what you want to do
And being imprisoned for being a prisoner.

What makes a poet bird sing in Sing Sing,
Beak ready to say absolutely anything?
The cage and the rage
And a future of old age
Make a squealer sing in Sing Sing.
That's what this admirer of yours is made of.

What surpasses being in love, unless it's love?
What's better than gardens and landscape?
Who described gardening as "the slowest of the performing arts"?
Who wrote about green grandeur?
Who rode to hounds over timber fences?
Who got thrown out of Foxcroft?

Dearest Grits, my beautiful powerhouse ex,
You goaded me into the happiness you guided me through.
Just saw Marco Island, Florida, on a map.
Remember the Christmas lights, the beach?
The Parthenon, the pink coat, the picnic
With Alzan in the olive grove,

Barbados, Ghana, the Hôtel Raphael, the Hôtel Lenox,
Les Gourcuff, snowy Sag Harbor,
Motorcycles in summer Sag Harbor.
Well, I don't often think back,
But right now I do. Mac, I too do,
By the light cast by you.

NEAR THE NEW WHITNEY

In the Meatpacking District,
Not far from the new Whitney,
In a charming restaurant,
I showed how charming I can be.
I showed how blue my eyes can be.
I showed I can be Dante first catching sight of Beatrice.

The maître d' was new to me.
The sudden sight of her, so gently lovely,
Threw me at the pressed-tin ceiling, where I stuck.
I asked her where I was, her name was Emily.
I don't know who the ceiling was.
I doubt pressed tin was what it was.

I was moonstruck.
Now I could only look up.
American art used to be risky.
American art used to be frisky
And drink a lot of whisky.
I looked up at Emily, not far from the new Whitney.

Seventy years ago,
There were violently drunkard painters downtown who,
Many of them, painted violently
In the Hamptons also.
Now they were in the splendid new Whitney, dead
Instead.

I wished I had a sled dog's beautiful eyes,
One blue, one brown,
To mush across the blizzard whiteout
Of sexy chirping chicks and well-trimmed
Bearded white young men.
You see how blue my old eyes aren't.

I drank an after-dinner tumbler of whisky
Not far from the new Whitney,
A present from the maître d'.
Sweet Lagavulin single malt filled me with infinity
Sixteen years old, while the girl
Smiled softly.

AUTUMN

A man walks briskly away from his body
And from feeling slightly sick on a blazingly fall day.
The sky is fresh perfection, without a cloud of illness.
The air is clean and cool as a fountain.
The heat of the last few weeks deflates.
The man walks as fast as he can up a mountain
In the middle of his head,
In the middle of a city.

Notwithstanding your attempts to indict me,
I will not fall ill, I refuse, he says.
He says, Some things are more delicious than other things,
Minister of doodle-y-doo,
Prince of sky after sky of blue.
Even in almost a drought,
Things can be succulent and full
And capable of merci beaucoup.

Sky after sky of blue, to match his eyes,
Is also the color he looks best in,
And also what these fall days have been so far, a fresh perfection.
A man should be wearing the sky.
A fellow should wear what he is walking under,
And when the day clouds over, especially so.
He's ready to travel via his smartphone to her gloriousness
Faster than the cars go in a Formula 1 race.

Behold his angel far away,
Who might as well be cocooned in outer space,
But in fact she's in a country where the sky is always gray,
And where the sky wants to stay that way.
If you make up your mind to,
You can be together in her weather.
Or if you'd rather,
And can't live without her, you can die.

Round head, round brain, jagged heart,
Your heart barnacled by too much . . .
A space traveler incapable of space travel,
Back from a failed mission,
Lands out at sea on the deck of a nuclear submarine
With armed warheads that has surfaced for this purpose.
It is a spectacular fall day, and the gorgeous air is dressed in blue,
And the worshiper turns to her neighbor and gives the kiss of peace.

The leaves will be falling soon to make things fresh and clean and new.
People walking their dogs bend down
To pick up after their dogs the dog doo,
People obeying a city ordinance they've finally got used to.
No one expected where they were heading.
They join hands at a worldwide wedding.
The police commissioner is there, the mayor.
On the steps, kilts are wailing bagpipes.

QUAND VOUS SEREZ BIEN VIEILLE

Fifty years from now you'll be my age
And old like me instead
Of young, and I'll be dead
And therefore won't be any good in bed,

But you won't either at that stage,
When your lunatic beauty will exist only on this page
From fifty years before, when it still could ravage
Me and turn a dainty Harvard man into a grunting savage

Who climbs a ladder through the stars to reach the moon,
And plucks at his laptop and it becomes a lute,
And writes an old man's poem of pursuit—
Earth rising to the moon to sing a saccharine tune

And leave below the geriatric horror of his appetite
And hide inside the moonlight high above the awful sight.

BARBARA EPSTEIN

Sometime near dawn, driving a stolen car
So fast I will never arrive,
Floating without a destination and without a license
Along the empty highways across the Mississippi from St. Louis,
Just the occasional big interstate truck's

Prong of headlights sticking into the dark
Through the misty summer odor of *to get away!*
At age fifteen, too young to drive or drink—
Is what I did a lot of, with a lot of drink,
And the driver's-side window open

To loll my head out to sniff the oncoming breeze like a dog,
Quaffing the opiate of the gigantic fields of Illinois,
Sucking in deep breaths of the husky
Thick bittersweet bituminous
Rising already at this early hour from the factory smokestacks

Of collapsing factories made of roseate bricks,
Ecstatic, as though of prednisone I had drunk,
And that cold black earth smell out in the boondocks.
And Vergil takes me by the hand as we descend
To meet the shades of Homer, Ovid, Horace, Lucan.

And I stop to give those greats a ride at dawn
And in their company at sunrise whoosh to wherever I belong
On wings of song.
How in the world does this connect to Barbara Epstein?
This is a way of bringing flowers to her shrine.

If I'm constantly stealing my father's cars, forever, she is forever
Founding co-editor of *The New York Review of Books*, and that's better—
Even though she nearly always canceled at the last minute
Every lunch date she ever made with anyone, or so it seemed!
One of the great editors

(And even in that wicked world everyone revered her)
Could be relied on to cancel
The lunch date with you she herself had made.
It was her *tic nerveux* to have to.
This is what happens when you think of someone no longer alive you love.

VERDANT VALLEY

The ringing telephone sobs to be picked up and when I do
It's someone I love but don't see anymore,
Calling from her car to ask
If I remember one of the beautiful places

In the world is
Verdant Valley in My Lady's Manor
In Maryland horse country which
We drove through together thirty years before

And she was driving through right now.
Mac Griswold, *you* were one of the most beautiful
Places in the world I ever saw and no doubt still are.
I picture you beautifully calling from your car.

Amalia Karabas, I am at a loss to surpass
The music of your name,
Itself a verdant valley to match your beauty.
The sound deserves a poem and will get one.

Caramba, Karabas! Imagine the joy and the blast—
The most beautiful woman in Queens
Is teaching her eighth-grade class!
Amalia is the curriculum! Karabas is the syllabus!

Seventy years ago, Raymond Sunderland, ten years old,
Emptied the school lunchroom with a foaming,
Thrashing, gnashing grand mal seizure and
Days later at home killed himself,

I don't know how, ten years old.
The thing he wanted most was attention
Which when he got it made him want to die,
St. Louis, 1946, Miss Rossman's School.

I pledge allegiance to the flag,
But Miss Rossman and Miss Schwaner rule
With a wooden pointer to thwack you with they never use.
Beautiful Mrs. Marshall has big breasts behind her blouse

And wears an FDR pince-nez.
Finally, I am old enough to walk to school,
Walking the back way through the tree-drenched private streets
To the concrete schoolyard where we play during recess.

Reading and 'riting and 'rithmetic
Toss and turn, yearn and burn.
We thrash and gnash—and explode with foam!
And need to go home.

I never knew Mrs. Marshall's first name was Pauline.
That didn't stop me from daydreaming about her even when
I was seated at my little desk right beneath her verdant valley
Standing there, who by now is dead, I suppose.

ONE OF THE BRIDESMAIDS

I am remembering the unforgettable.
How the father of the bride
Took me aside
To say he knew I had vomited all over the chintz.

I hadn't—but desperately needed to escape
And took a borrowed car late at night out
On the dirt roads and silent highways of Westchester, drunk,
And got more and more utterly lost.

I had said to the best man, the groom's older brother,
That I would not be giving a toast, who said OK, perfectly all right,
And then called on me
To give the first toast.

My shocked toast was so brief
I sat down almost before I spoke.
There was an awkward tuxedo silence
While the room tried to figure out what had happened.

There I was in my drunken car
Looking for, somehow, *somewhere*—
Driving away from the wedding nightmare
Through the sweet night air.

I found a pay phone.
She said she would come and guide me back.
Who is this miracle arriving in her Corvette winged chariot—
And all of a sudden it's dawn!—softly saying: *Follow me, I'll lead the way?*

HYMN TO APHRODITE

Ποικιλόθρον᾽ α᾽Θανάτ᾽ Αφρόδιτα

—Sappho, *Fragment 1*

I gather you were in the lobby
Minutes before.
Terrifying to almost see you again.
I smelled the shockwave, the burning air.

You were too sexual
To be bourgeois, screams from the jungle
On top of Mount Olympus.
You were too violently beautiful.

Last night I looked up at the sky,
Lights out as I was falling asleep.
There was the moon, a full moon, or nearly.
It was you.

I wasn't, but I could have been,
A god I was living in.
I chose not to come out
On stage and tell them what a poem is about.

Pubic hair that befits a goddess.
Pubic hair that equips a goddess.
That little arrowhead of pubic hair that
Magnifies your thighs' magnificence.

You look like a field of flowers.
You look like flowers in a vase.
You look like brains and breasts.
You act like life stabbing death to death.

I'm packing heat. That's a poem. My concealed
Carry permit is revealed.
I do what I do.
Peaches goes it alone.

I was like a god or
I was like the tiny hermit crab
Who walks around inside a borrowed empty shell
Bigger than he is for protection.

I carry the shell
I've borrowed like an umbrella
Wherever I go
Along the shore.

I dress up in one of my million-dollar suits.
I scuttle along Broadway,
Ready to be found out and eaten
Naked.

A thunderbolt from you
Walks through my front door
And knocks me to the floor
Where you and I, in love, still are

On top of Mount Olympus
Screaming your eternal estrus,
Eyes white and blank with blind
Ecstatic lack of sight.

THE BLUE SUIT

Richard Anderson, master Savile Row tailor,
Opens the eleventh-floor hotel room door
Wearing a new suit so blue
It makes me smile,
Something no suit has been able to do for quite a while.
Welcome to room 1111 at the Carlyle.

When earlier in the morning Richard crossed the street
To the pharmacy opposite,
A stranger coming out of Zitomer's cried out,
"My God, that suit is *blue*!"
Which was hilariously true.
All day long people remarked on it: the suit, and the blue, and the fit.

Richard and I walk around with, in our heads, a museum
Of, in his case, clothes he has made over the years,
And, in mine, clothes he has made for me that I have worn.
I have worn a lot of clothes since I was born.
Diapers eventually turned into bespoke
Suits that rise like ghosts out of the smoke.

Suits hang from their hangers in my mind
And faintly tinkle in the wind
Like wind chimes,
Prettifying my many crimes.
Mr. Hall at Huntsman was followed by his former pupil,
Now at his own firm, Richard Anderson at Richard Anderson.

What does a blue suit do?
What does a blue suit know?
It won't find friends in Moscow
When it's as electric blue as this one is.
It's a bit too Broadway musical, too Broadway show,
For Washington, D.C.

My dear severe Mr. Hall, whom I called the Reverend,
And who died a decade ago,
Wafts like mist through my mind
And falls like gently falling snow.
The wind chimes tinkle softly in the perfumed nights on Bali.
The trumpets of life-after-death blow.

SURF'S UP

Nothing to write home about.
No home to write home to.
Oh boohoo! I've never heard
Anything so disgustingly absurd.
The snow is falling crazily outside the window.

Now it's spring.
Still cold but the little birds this morning began to sing.
But the fucking pigeons are a constant curse.
Disgusting and absurd moans of human sexual intercourse
On the ledge outside my study window.

I'm leaping without wings,
Though I wouldn't mind having wings,
To you.
I'm leaping out my window to you.
Right through the screen of my computer into

Women don't like us anymore
And hold meeting after meeting over what to do.
Surf's up!
They ride the big wave.
They're not why the planet may be doomed.

Picture a scene right out of Disney Classics of giant saguaro cactuses,
Enormous nude green hairless tubes with arms
That look like prehistory reaching out without hands.
I hear the goddamned pigeons making a baby.
We share a desert.

What are you looking at?
I dug and dug to get out
A contact lens that it turned out wasn't in my eye
And got instead a ghoulish
Eyeball of blood.

It didn't hurt and I could see just fine,
Though it looked as if one eye was slowly cooking in red wine.
When I see your tits on FaceTime I see stars.
I see Stars and Stripes and Stars and Bars.
I'm in the finally-escaping-with-the-human-species-to-Mars

Mode, winged but without wings, coldcocked by love, out cold, surf's up.
Get into your Skype outfit.
Prepare for departure from this planet.
The last standing naked saguaros stand
There in the desert inside the Carlyle Hotel lobby.

I look in the men's room mirror at a man and his blood thinner.
Why, it's you, Eliquis, dear friend!
I see myself for a fleeting second looking like someone else.
I like the tiny Cartier watch the fellow's wearing.
I remember when he was once in Tahiti.

Lift me off the ground, mighty Ezra Pound!
Sing me your lyrical skunk spray of Cantos.
Robert Lowell, I will join you soon.
I remember DVF's enchantment apartment in the Rue de Seine.
I remember Mumbai when it was Bombay.

England—where the English are—
Used to smile with bad English teeth in the toxic coal-fires air.
It was the London of T. S. Eliot,
St. Louisan and expatriate,
Who found love late.

Index of Titles
and First Lines